THE TYRANNY OF METRICS

THE
TYRANNY
OF
METRICS

JERRY Z. MULLER

PRINCETON UNIVERSITY PRESS
PRINCETON & OXFORD

Copyright © 2018 by Princeton University Press

Published by Princeton University Press,
41 William Street, Princeton, New Jersey 08540

In the United Kingdom: Princeton University Press,
6 Oxford Street, Woodstock, Oxfordshire OX20 1TR

press.princeton.edu

Jacket design by Chris Ferrante

Book epigraph from *Everything: A Book of Aphorisms*, 2nd ed., by Aaron Haspel.
Copyright © 2015 by Aaron Haspel. Published by Good Books and reprinted here
by permission of the author.

All Rights Reserved

ISBN 978-0-691-17495-2

British Library Cataloging-in-Publication Data is available

This book has been composed in Sabon Next, Alternate Gothic, and Gotham

Printed on acid-free paper. ∞

Printed in the United States of America

10 9 8 7 6 5 4 3 2 1

FOR PETER J. DOUGHERTY

"Those who believe that what you cannot quantify does not exist also believe that what you can quantify, does."

—AARON HASPEL

CONTENTS

THE TYRANNY OF METRICS

INTRODUCTION

Based on the real-life experiences of its creators, David Simon and Ed Burns, the HBO series *The Wire* is regarded by some as among the greatest cultural documents of our age. And with good reason. Focused on a single American city, Baltimore, the series drills down into a few major institutions—the police, the school system, municipal politics, the press—and provides an X-ray–like image of their workings and dysfunctions. The series has attracted an international audience because its themes of organizational dysfunction resonate broadly across Western societies.

One of the recurrent themes of *The Wire* is the salience of metrics: of measured performance as the hallmark of "accountability." Police commanders are obsessed with hitting the numbers—for example, cases solved, drug arrests, crime rates—and they do so by a variety of means that sacrifice effectiveness to meeting statistical targets. Politicians demand numbers that attest to police success in controlling crime. So the police units do their best to avoid having murders attributed to their district: when it turns out that a drug gang has been disposing of bodies in abandoned houses, the homicide sergeant discourages their discovery, since that would diminish the "clearance rate," the metric of the percentage of crimes solved. Much of the plot revolves around dedicated detectives seeking to develop a complex criminal case against a major drug lord. But since building that case will take months if not years, they are discouraged from doing so by the higher-ups, who want the cops to rack up favorable metrics by arresting lots of low-level drug dealers, despite the fact that those arrested will be replaced almost instantly. The mayor's office demands that the rate of major crimes decline by 5 percent before the end of the year, a target that can be reached only by overlooking actual crimes or downgrading their seriousness. In each case, they are engaged in "juking the stats"—improving their metrics either by distorting actual results, or by diverting their time and effort from crime prevention to less productive work.

Another plot line involves an ex-cop who teaches in a middle school in a neighborhood plagued by poverty, drug abuse, and family fragmentation. Students in the school perform poorly, and the school is in danger of being closed if the test scores of its students do not improve. So, in the six weeks before the standardized English reading and writing tests are to be administered, the teachers are instructed by their principal to focus all of class time on practicing for the tests, ignoring other subjects entirely (a strategy euphemistically referred to as "curriculum alignment"). "Teaching to the test," like juking the stats, is a way in which institutions are perverted, as effort is diverted from the institution's true purpose (education) to meeting the metric targets on which its survival has come to depend.

The distortive effects of performance metrics are felt at least as much across the Atlantic, in Great Britain.[1] There, another television series penned by a former real-life practitioner captures the same phenomenon. The series, *Bodies*, written by Jed Mercurio, a former hospital physician, takes place in the obstetrics and gynecology ward of a metropolitan hospital. In the first episode, a newly arrived senior surgeon performs an operation on a patient with complex comorbidities, after which she dies. His rival then provides him with this advice: "The superior surgeon uses his superior judgment to steer clear of any situation that might test his superior ability." That is, he avoids difficult cases as a way of maintaining his success rate. A classic strategy of "creaming," that is, avoiding risky instances that might have a negative impact on one's measured performance. The cost of this tactic is that patients at greater risk for a failed surgery are left to an almost certain death without surgery.

Bodies is a medical drama, but the phenomena it depicts exist in the real world. Numerous studies have shown that when surgeons, for example, are rated or remunerated according to their success rates, some respond by refusing to operate on patients with more complex or critical conditions. Excluding the more difficult cases—those that involve the likelihood of poorer outcomes—improves the surgeons' success rates, and hence their metrics, their reputation, and their remuneration. That of course comes at the expense of the excluded patients, who pay with their lives. But those deaths do not show up in the metrics.

As we'll see, gaming the metrics occurs in every realm: in policing; in primary, secondary, and higher education; in medicine; in nonprofit organizations; and, of course, in business. And gaming is only one class of problems that inevitably arise when using performance metrics as the basis of reward or sanction. There are things that can be measured. There are things that are worth measuring. But what can be measured is not always what is worth measuring; what gets measured may have no relationship to what we really want to know. The costs of measuring may be greater than the benefits. The things that get measured may draw effort away from the things we really care about. And measurement may provide us with distorted knowledge—knowledge that seems solid but is actually deceptive.

We live in the age of measured accountability, of reward for measured performance, and belief in the virtues of publicizing those metrics through "transparency." But the identification of accountability with metrics and with transparency is deceptive. Accountability ought to mean being held responsible for one's actions. But by a sort of linguistic sleight of hand, accountability has come to mean demonstrating success through standardized measurement, as if only that which can be counted really counts. Another assumption that is often taken for granted is that "accountability" demands that measurement of performance be made public, that is, "transparent."

The metric fixation is the seemingly irresistible pressure to measure performance, to publicize it, and to reward it, often in the face of evidence that this just doesn't work very well.

Used properly, measurement, as we'll see, can be a good thing. So can transparency. But they can also distort, divert, displace, distract, and discourage. While we are bound to live in an age of measurement, we live in an age of mismeasurement, over-measurement, misleading measurement, and counterproductive measurement. This book is not about the evils of measuring. It is about the unintended negative consequences of trying to substitute standardized measures of performance for personal judgment based on experience. The problem is not measurement, but excessive measurement and inappropriate measurement—not metrics, but metric fixation.

We are often told that gathering metrics of measured performance and then making them available to the public is a way to improve the functioning of our institutions. Nowhere have the virtues of accountability, performance metrics, and transparency been more touted than in the field of medicine. And understandably so, for nowhere are the stakes higher. The health sector not only makes up over 17 percent of the U.S. economy, but lives are also on the line. Surely, the logic goes, measures of performance can help save dollars and save lives.

Gathering standardized information about the success rates of surgeons, or the survival rate of patients admitted to particular hospitals, is supposed to be helpful. For if doctors or hospitals are remunerated by government agencies or private insurers based on their success rates in keeping patients alive, then such measurements should create incentives for better care. And if the success rates of doctors and hospitals are publicized, the resulting transparency will allow the public to choose among doctors and among hospitals. All in all, metrics, accountability, and transparency will provide the cure for what ails the medical professions. What could go wrong?

A good deal, as we have already seen. When their scores are used as a basis of reward and punishment, surgeons, as do others under such scrutiny, engage in creaming, that is, they avoid the riskier cases. When hospitals are penalized based on the percentage of patients who fail to survive for thirty days beyond surgery, patients are sometimes kept alive for thirty-one days, so that their mortality is not reflected in the hospital's metrics.[2] In England, in an attempt to reduce wait times in emergency wards, the Department of Health adopted a policy that penalized hospitals with wait times longer than four hours. The program succeeded—at least on the surface. In fact, some hospitals responded by keeping incoming patients in queues of ambulances, beyond the doors of the hospital, until the staff was confident that the patient could be seen within the allotted four hours of being admitted.[3]

We'll explore these issues in the realm of medicine in greater depth. But what is striking is that the problems that arise in healthcare arise in many other institutions—in K-12 and college education; in policing and other public services; in business and finance; and in charitable organizations. Those who work in any of these fields will have some sense of such problems in their institutions. And social scientists have examined and anatomized them in one or another of these realms. What has gone largely unnoticed is the recurrence of the same unintended negative consequences of performance metrics, accountability, and transparency across a wide range of institutions.[4]

As with many insights, once you've become aware of metric fixation, you are likely to find it almost everywhere—and not just in television dramas.

The catchwords of metric fixation are all around us. Google's Ngram—which instantly searches through thousands of scanned books and other publications—provides a rough but telling portrait of changes in our culture and society. Set the parameters by years, type in a term or phrase, and up pops a graph showing the incidence of the words from 1800 to the present. Type in "accountability" and you will see a line that begins to curve upward around 1965, with an increasingly rising slope after 1985. So too with "metrics," which begins its steep increase around 1985. "Benchmarks" follows the same pattern, as does "performance indicators."

This book argues that while they are a potentially valuable tool, the virtues of accountability metrics have been oversold, and their costs are often underappreciated. It offers an etiology and diagnosis, but also a prognosis for how metric fixation can be avoided, and its pains alleviated.

The most characteristic feature of metric fixation is the aspiration to replace judgment based on experience with standardized measurement. For judgment is understood as personal, subjective, and self-interested. Metrics, by contrast, are supposed to provide information that is hard and objective. The strategy is to improve institutional efficiency by offering rewards to those whose metrics are highest, or whose benchmarks or targets have been reached, and to penalize those who fall behind. Policies based on these assumptions have been on the march for several decades, and as the ever-rising slope of the Ngram graphs indicate, their assumed truth goes marching on.

To be sure, there are many situations where decision-making based on standardized measurement is superior to judgment based upon personal experience and expertise. Decisions based on big data are useful when the experience of any single practitioner is likely to be too limited to develop an intuitive feel for or reliable measure of efficacy. When a physician confronts the symptoms of a rare disorder, for example, she is better advised to rely on standardized criteria based on the aggregation of many cases. Checklists—standardized procedures for how to proceed under routine conditions—have been shown to be valuable in fields as varied as airlines and medicine.[5] And, as recounted in the book *Moneyball*, statistical analysis can sometimes discover that clearly measureable but neglected characteristics are more significant than is recognized by intuitive understanding based on accumulated experience.[6]

Used judiciously, then, measurement of the previously unmeasured can provide real benefits. The attempt to measure performance—while pocked with pitfalls, as we will see—is intrinsically desirable. If what is *actually* measured is a reasonable proxy for what is *intended* to be measured, and if it is combined with judgment, then measurement can help practitioners to assess their own performance, both for individuals and for organizations. But problems arise when such measures become the criteria used to reward and punish—when metrics become the basis of pay-for-performance or ratings.

Schemes of measured performance are deceptively attractive because they often "prove" themselves by spotting the most egregious cases of error or neglect, but are then applied to all cases. Tools appropriate for discovering real misconduct become tools for measuring all performance. The initial findings of performance measurement may lead poor performers to improve, or to drop out of the market. But in many cases, the extension of standardized measurement may be of diminishing utility, or even counterproductive—sliding from sensible solutions to metric madness. Above all, measurement may become counterproductive when it tries to measure the unmeasurable and quantify the unquantifiable.

Concrete interests of power, money, and status are at stake. Metric fixation leads to a diversion of resources away from frontline producers toward managers, administrators, and those who gather and manipulate data.

When metrics are used by managers as a tool to control professionals, it often creates a tension between the managers who seek to measure and reward performance, and the ethos of the professionals (doctors, nurses, policemen, teachers, professors, etc.). The professional ethos is based on mastery of a body of specialized knowledge acquired through an extended process of education and training; autonomy and control over work; an identification with one's professional group and a sense of responsibility toward colleagues; a high valuation of intrinsic rewards; and a commitment to the interests of clients above considerations of cost.[7]

That tension is sometimes necessary and desirable, for the professional ethos tends to discount issues of cost and opportunity cost. That is, the professional is inclined to see only the advantages of providing more of his or her services, without much attention to the limits of resources, or their alternate uses. Professionals don't like to think about costs. Metrics folks do. When the two groups work together, the result can be greater satisfaction for both. When they are pitted against one another, the result is conflict and declining morale.

While there are vested interests at stake that sometimes lead from reasonable metrics to metric madness, the cause lies as much in the uncritical adoption of metric ideology. Like every culture, the culture of metric accountability has its own unquestioned sacred terms and its characteristic blind spots.[8] Yet today it is so dominant that its flaws tend to go unnoticed.

You might wonder how a historian came to write a book about the tyranny of metrics. It happened as I came to recognize that troubling developments in my own professional experience were reflections of much larger patterns in our society. Microlevel discontents led to macrolevel analysis, as I came to understand that cultural patterns that were damaging my narrow professional turf were warping many contemporary institutions.

I was drawn into the subject through my experience as the chair of my department at a private university. There are many facets to such a job: mentoring faculty members to help them develop as scholars and teachers; hiring new faculty; trying to ensure that necessary courses get taught; maintaining relations with deans and others in the university administration. Those responsibilities were on top of my roles as a faculty member: teaching, researching, and keeping up with my professional fields. With all those roles, I was quite satisfied. Time devoted to thinking about and working with faculty members contributed to making them better teachers and scholars. I was proud of the range and quality of the courses that we were teaching, and relations with other departments were fine. Teaching, researching, and writing were demanding, but satisfying.

Then, things began to change. Like all colleges and universities, our institution gets evaluated every decade by an accrediting body, the Middle States Commission on Higher Education. It issued a report that included demands for more metrics on which to base future "assessment"—a buzzword in higher education that usually means more measurement of performance. Soon, I found my time increasingly devoted to answering queries for more and more statistical information about the activities of the department, which diverted my time from tasks such as research, teaching, and mentoring faculty. There were new scales for evaluating the achievements of our graduating majors—scales that added no useful insights to our previous measuring instrument, namely grades. I worked out a way of doing this speedily, without taking up much time of the faculty, simply by translating the grades the faculty had awarded into the four-category scale created for purposes of assessment. Over time, gathering and processing the information, in turn, required the university to hire ever more data specialists. (It has since gone so far as to appoint a vice-president for assessment.) Some of their reports were genuinely useful: for example, in producing spreadsheets that showed the average grade awarded in each course. But much of the information was of no real use, and indeed, was read by no one. Yet once the culture of performance documentation caught on, department chairs found themselves in a sort of data arms race. I led the department through a required year-long departmental self-assessment—a useful exercise, as it turned out. But before sending it up the bureaucratic chain, I was urged to add more statistical appendices—because if I didn't, the report would look less rigorous than that of other departments. One fellow chair—a solid senior scholar—devoted most of one summer to compiling a binder full of data, complete with colored charts, to try to convince the dean of the need to fill a faculty slot in his department.

My experience was irritating, not shattering: a pin-prick not a blow. But it stimulated me to inquire more deeply into the forces leading to this wasteful diversion of time and effort. The Middle States Commission, from which the stimulus for more data originated, operates with a mandate from the U.S. Department of Education. That department, under the leadership of Margaret Spellings, had convened a Commission on the Future of Higher Education, which published its report in 2006 emphasizing the need for greater accountability and the gathering of more data, and directing the regional accrediting agencies to make "performance outcomes" the core of their assessment.[9] That mode of evaluation, in turn, filtered down to the Middle States Commission, and from there to the administration of my university, and eventually down to me. Spellings had been the director of the Domestic Policy Council under President George W. Bush at the time of the passage of the No Child Left Behind Act in 2001. At first, I had thought that legislation—which expanded the evaluation of teachers and schools based on the scores of their students on standardized tests—was a positive step. But in time I came to hear searing critiques of it by erstwhile supporters, such as the former assistant secretary of education, Diane Ravitch. And classroom teachers of my acquaintance told me that while they loved teaching, they found that the increasing regimentation of the curriculum, intended to maximize performance on the tests, was sucking away their enthusiasm.

Such accounts led me to investigate, using my own intellectual toolkit, the broader historical and cultural roots and contemporary manifestations of the culture of measured and rewarded performance that is permeating ever more institutions. My professional interests had been on the borders between history, economics, sociology, and politics. I had long been interested in the history of what we have come to call "public policy," and had published a book on Adam Smith as a public policy analyst. I had also written about the history of conservative approaches to public policy, and some of the thinkers I had written about, such as Michael Oakeshott and Friedrich Hayek, turned out to provide critical insights into our contemporary apotheosis of measured performance. I had been interested in the history of capitalism, especially the ways in which intellectuals have thought about the social, moral, and political prerequisites and ramifications of business. A recurrent concern among modern Western intellectuals about whom I had written was the potentially pernicious spillover effects of concepts and predispositions from business and from the discipline of economics into other realms of life. And so, my personal experience of professional discontent proved serendipitous, stimulating me to investigations that drew upon a wide range of my interests. The spirits presiding over this book are those of Matthew Arnold, the great Victorian cultural critic, and of my teacher, Robert K. Merton, who schooled me to look out for the unanticipated and unintended consequences of social action—and for serendipity in scholarship.[10]

As I began to investigate these issues, a book by a sociologist at the Harvard Business School, Rakesh Khurana's *From Higher Aims to Hired Hands: The Social Transformation of American Business Schools and the Unfulfilled Promise of Management as a Profession*, opened my eyes to the intellectual history of business schools themselves, and the broader impact of what gets taught in them. These insights led me to wider investigations of the changing culture and ideologies in the field of management, the sometimes dubious nature of which is nicely captured in the title of Adrian Wooldridge's book, *The Witch Doctors* (a second edition carries the more benign title, *Masters of Management*).

I proceeded to consult a wide range of scholarly literatures, in fields from economics and politics, to history, anthropology, psychology, sociology, public administration, and organizational behavior. I made extensive use of social scientific studies of the actual behavior of teachers, professors, doctors, and policemen in the real world.

In surveying the scholarship on the topic from a variety of fields, I was struck by the degree to which academic disciplines tend to be walled off from one another, and by the gap between academic research and real world practice. I found remarkable, for example, how much of recent economic literature on incentives and motivation was a formalization of what psychologists had already discovered. But much of what psychologists had discovered was long known by managers with judgment. Yet although there is a large body of scholarship in the fields of psychology and economics that call into question the premises and effectiveness of pay for measured performance, that literature seems to have done little to halt the spread of metric fixation.[11]

That is why I wrote this book. Little of what this book has to say is entirely new—it is based on synthesizing research and insights drawn from many other authors. Many of the dysfunctions connected with what I've termed "metric fixation" have been documented and analyzed by scholars writing about one or another domain: education, medicine, policing, profit-oriented enterprises, and nonprofits. A few students of organizational behavior, writing in rather specialized venues, have analyzed some of the broader patterns of success and dysfunction. What no one has really done is put it all together and make it accessible to all of us who guide and work in these institutions, from politicians deciding on the fate of educational and medical systems, to members of boards of directors of corporations, to trustees of universities and nonprofit organizations, and down to the peons (such as department chairs). This book is for them. More broadly, it's for anyone who wants to understand one of the big reasons why so many contemporary organizations function less well than they ought to, diminishing productivity while frustrating those who work in them.

Though the thrust of the argument rubs against the received wisdom of many contemporary institutions, I've aimed not at novelty but at distilled wisdom. Readers eager to pigeonhole the argument into some existing ideological framework will be disappointed, as it draws not only from a variety of disciplines but from a variety of political orientations. I have drawn upon evidence and insight from wherever they were to be found. I hope that readers will approach the book with the same open mind.

THE ARGUMENT

THE ARGUMENT IN A NUTSHELL

There is a cultural pattern that has become ubiquitous in recent decades, engulfing an ever-widening range of institutions. Depending on taste, one could call it a cultural "meme," an "épistème," a "discourse," a "paradigm," a "self-reinforcing rhetorical system,"[1] or simply a fashion. It comes with its own vocabulary and master terms. It affects the way in which people *talk* about the world, and thus how they *think* about the world and how they *act* in it.[2] For convenience, let's call it metric fixation.

A key premise of metric fixation concerns the relationship between measurement and improvement. There is a dictum (wrongly) attributed to the great nineteenth-century physicist Lord Kelvin: "If you cannot measure it, you cannot improve it." In 1986 the American management guru, Tom Peters, embraced the motto, "What gets measured gets done," which became a cornerstone belief of metrics.[3] In time, some drew the conclusion that "anything that can be measured can be improved."[4]

When proponents of metrics advocate "accountability," they tacitly combine two meanings of the word. On the one hand, to be accountable means to be responsible. But it can also mean "capable of being counted." Advocates of "accountability" typically assume that only by counting can institutions be truly responsible. Performance is therefore equated with what can be reduced to standardized measurements.

When proponents of metrics demand "transparency" they often insinuate that probity requires making explicit and visible as much information as possible. The result is the demand for ever more documentation, ever more mission statements, ever more "goal-setting."[5]

The key components of metric fixation are

- the belief that it is possible and desirable to replace judgment, acquired by personal experience and talent, with numerical indicators of comparative performance based upon standardized data (metrics);
- the belief that making such metrics public (transparent) assures that institutions are actually carrying out their purposes (accountability);
- the belief that the best way to motivate people within these organizations is by attaching rewards and penalties to their measured performance, rewards that are either monetary (pay-for-performance) or reputational (rankings).

Metric fixation is the persistence of these beliefs despite their unintended negative consequences when they are put into practice.[6] It occurs because not everything that is important is measureable, and much that is measurable is unimportant. (Or, in the words of a familiar dictum, "Not everything that can be counted counts, and not everything that counts can be counted."[7]) Most organizations have multiple purposes, and that which is measured and rewarded tends to become the focus of attention, at the expense of other essential goals. Similarly, many jobs have multiple facets, and measuring only a few aspects creates incentives to neglect the rest.[8] When organizations committed to metrics wake up to this fact, they typically add more performance measures—which creates a cascade of data, data that becomes ever less useful, while gathering it sucks up more and more time and resources.

In the process, the nature of work is transformed in ways that are often pernicious. Professionals tend to resent the impositions of goals that may conflict with their vocational ethos and judgment, and thus morale is lowered. Almost inevitably, many people become adept at manipulating performance indicators through a variety of methods, many of which are ultimately dysfunctional for their organizations. They fudge the data or deal only with cases that will improve performance indicators. They fail to report negative instances. In extreme cases, they fabricate the evidence.

A frequent feature of metric fixation is paying for performance, that is, offering individuals or organizations financial incentives to meet quantifiable criteria. That may work in organizations that exist for the single purpose of making a profit, though as we'll see, even in these cases it is rarely effective. It works even less well in organizations in which employees are oriented to a more idealistic mission, such as schools, universities, medical practices, and hospitals. Whenever reward is tied to measured performance, metric fixation invites gaming.

Because the theory of motivation behind pay for measured performance is stunted, results are often at odds with expectations. The typical pattern of dysfunction was formulated in 1975 by two social scientists operating on opposite sides of the Atlantic, in what appears to have been a case of independent discovery. What has come to be called "Campbell's Law," named for the American social psychologist Donald T. Campbell, holds that "[t]he more any quantitative social indicator is used for social decision-making, the more subject it will be to corruption pressures and the more apt it will be to distort and corrupt the social processes it is intended to monitor."[9]

In a variation named for the British economist who formulated it, we have Goodhart's Law, which states, "Any measure used for control is unreliable."[10] To put it another way, anything that can be measured and rewarded will be gamed. We will see many variations on this theme.

Trying to force people to conform their work to preestablished numerical goals tends to stifle innovation and creativity—valuable qualities in most settings. And it almost inevitably leads to a valuation of short-term goals over long-term purposes.

In situations where there are no real feasible solutions to a problem, the gathering and publication of performance data serves as a form of virtue signaling. There is no real progress to show, but the effort demonstrated in gathering and publicizing the data satisfies a sense of moral earnestness. In lieu of real progress, the progress of measurement becomes a simulacrum of success. We'll see that in the case of the educational "achievement gap."

Because belief in its efficacy seems to outlast evidence that it frequently doesn't work, metric fixation has elements of a cult. Studies that demonstrate its lack of effectiveness are either ignored, or met with the assertion that what is needed is more data and better measurement. Metric fixation, which aspires to imitate science, too often resembles faith.

All of that is not intended to claim that measurement is useless or intrinsically pernicious. One of the purposes of this book is to specify when performance metrics are genuinely useful—how to use metrics without the characteristic dysfunctions of metric fixation.

The next chapter, "Recurring Flaws," provides a taxonomy of the most frequent types of flaws in the use of performance metrics. Defining and labeling them will make it easier to refer back to them later. Then, in part II, we examine the origins of metric fixation and account for its spread and tenacity in spite of its frequent failures, in addition to exploring some of the deeper philosophical sources of its shortcomings. Part III comprises case studies that examine the more recent record of metrics, it successes and its shortcomings in a variety of fields, including K-12 education, higher education, medicine, policing, the military, business, and philanthropy and foreign aid. These case studies are intended to be suggestive rather than definitive. That is, they don't deal with every way in which the metric fixation manifests itself in each domain. Rather they provide concrete examples of recurring flaws and unintended consequences, as well as examples of the successful use of metrics from which we may derive lessons that can be applied in other domains. This section is followed by a brief excursus on the theme of transparency as the enemy of performance in certain realms. Finally, Part IV draws upon the preceding analysis to enumerate the unintended negative consequences of metric fixation and offer some guidelines about when and how to make use of metrics without succumbing to metric fixation.

RECURRING FLAWS

The drive to institute metrics often arises from the best of intentions, as a purported solution to real problems. And in some cases, as we'll see, it really *does* fulfill its promise to provide such solutions, or at least contributes to solving problems. But after decades of experience with the negative effects of metrics, as metric dysfunction threatens to cascade into yet more institutions, we should be able to anticipate the recurrent flaws. Here's a list to help identify and remember them. Of course, while we may distinguish them for purposes of analysis, these flaws often overlap in the real world.

Let's begin with problems of the *distortion* of information.

Measuring the most easily measurable. There is a natural human tendency to try to simplify problems by focusing on the most easily measureable elements.[1] But what is most easily measured is rarely what is most important, indeed sometimes not important at all. That is the first source of metric dysfunction.

Closely related is **measuring the simple when the desired outcome is complex.** Most jobs have multiple responsibilities and most organizations have multiple goals. Focusing measurement on just one responsibility or goal often leads to deceptive results.

Measuring inputs rather than outcomes. It is often easier to measure the amount spent or the resources injected into a project than the *results* of the efforts. So organizations measure what they've spent, rather than what they produce, or they measure process rather than product.

Degrading information quality through standardization. Quantification is seductive, because it organizes and simplifies knowledge. It offers numerical information that allows for easy comparison among people and institutions.[2] But that simplification may lead to distortion, since making things comparable often means that they are stripped of their context, history, and meaning.[3] The result is that the information appears more certain and authoritative than is actually the case: the caveats, the ambiguities, and uncertainties are peeled away, and nothing does more to create the appearance of certain knowledge than expressing it in numerical form.[4]

Campbell's Law and Goodhart's Law are warnings about the inevitable attempts to game the metric when much is at stake. Gaming the metrics takes a variety of forms.

Gaming through creaming. This takes place when practitioners find simpler targets or prefer clients with less challenging circumstances, making it easier to reach the metric goal, but excluding cases where success is more difficult to achieve.

Improving numbers by lowering standards. One way of improving metric scores is by lowering the criteria for scoring. Thus, for example, graduation rates of high schools and colleges can be increased by lowering the standards for passing. Or airlines improve their on-time performance by increasing the scheduled flying time of their flights.

Improving numbers through omission or distortion of data. This strategy involves leaving out inconvenient instances, or classifying cases in a way that makes them disappear from the metrics. Police forces can "reduce" crime rates by booking felonies as misdemeanors, or by deciding not to book reported crimes at all.

Cheating. One step beyond gaming the metrics is cheating— a phenomenon whose frequency tends to increase directly with the stakes of the metric in question. As we'll see, as the No Child Left Behind Act raised the stakes for schools of the test scores of their pupils, teachers and principals in many cities responded by altering students' answers on the test.

BACKGRO

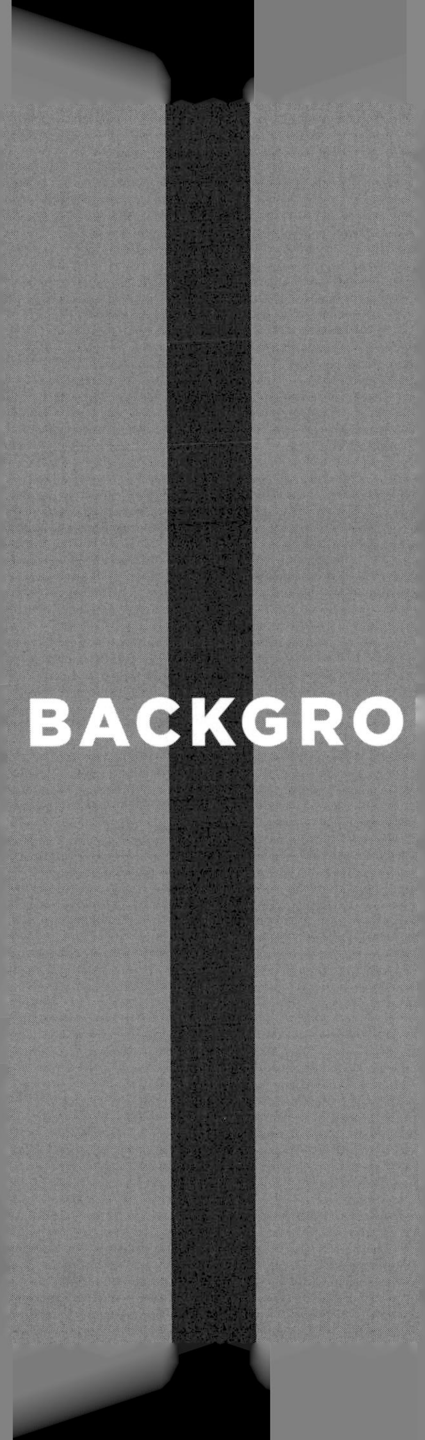

THE ORIGINS OF MEASURING AND PAYING FOR PERFORMANCE

"Accountability," "metrics," and "performance indicators" have become cultural memes. Embracing them promises a seat on the train of historical progress, and no politician, agency chief, university president, or school superintendent wants to be left behind. When metrics becomes the coin of the realm, to refuse to use it is to risk bankruptcy. There is pressure from elected officials and from foundation managers to pay up.

How and why did this tyranny of metrics come about?

SOME ORIGINS OF PAYING FOR MEASURED PERFORMANCE

The idea that organizations outside the free market would be more efficient if they were paid based on measured performance seems to have occurred first to policymakers in Victorian Britain. In 1862, Robert Lowe, a Liberal member of parliament who oversaw the committee on education, proposed a new method for government funding of schools, which would be based on "payment by results." Lowe had distinguished himself in 1856 by shepherding through parliament a seminal piece of legislation in the history of capitalism. That was the Joint Stock Companies Act, which, together with legislation passed the previous year, the Limited Liability Act, set out a new law for corporations based on the principal of limited liability. From reforming the structure of business, Lowe turned to reforming government-supported schools.

Lowe's scheme was based on the premise that "the duty of a State in public education is . . . to obtain the greatest possible quantity of reading, writing, and arithmetic for the greatest number."[1] Schools were to be funded based on the performance of their students in the "3 Rs." Each school was to be visited annually by a school inspector, who was to quiz every student in English language and arithmetic. For every student who failed to appear or to answer questions successfully, a small sum would be deducted from the school's government funding. Lowe's reform was intended in part to cut costs, but above all to make school funding dependent on measurable results in the most basic and practical of skills, and to bring education into accord with his market-oriented principles by linking payment to performance.[2]

Lowe's scheme was challenged by Matthew Arnold, the great cultural critic, whose day job was as a government inspector of the very schools Lowe set out to transform. Arnold warned consistently against extending the criteria appropriate to the market to other areas of life. With a dose of bravery, Arnold launched a public salvo against his political superior. In an essay entitled "The Twice-Revised Code," Arnold attacked the narrow and mechanical conception of education implied by the code. The ability to read intelligently, he pointed out, developed primarily not from narrowly tailored reading lessons, but from a more general cultivation, imbibed from the family or, failing that, from a school environment that created the mental desire to read. The goal of the schools, therefore, should be "general intellectual cultivation," without which the skills of reading and writing would not develop.[3] The government, he lamented, sought to fund only the most rudimentary of educations instead of responding to "the strong desire of the lower classes to raise themselves."[4] Since many impoverished students would inevitably be absent when the annual test was administered, or would fail the test itself, he predicted that the net effect of the proposed reform would be to reduce the funding of schools for the poor. The education of the people, he concluded, was to be sacrificed to "the friends of economy at any price."[5]

Arnold frequently found himself inspecting schools where students ingested mountains of facts and arithmetic, but were bereft of analytic ability and utterly incapable of understanding sophisticated prose or poetry. They were taught not to reason but to cram.[6] Both before and especially after the adoption of "payment for performance," he criticized such education for being "far too little formative and humanizing ... much in it, which its administrators point to as valuable *results*, is in truth mere machinery."[7] This conception of education as machinery, tailored to the measurable production of reading, writing, and computation, and capable of being rewarded based on measurable output, ebbed and flowed in the decades that followed, reaching a flood tide at the end of the twentieth century.

At each subsequent wave, we'll encounter critics like Arnold, who pointed to the unmeasured costs of tying reward to standardized measurement.

MEASURING PERFORMANCE: TAYLORISM

There were traces of metric fixation in the school efficiency movement that rolled across the American educational landscape, starting in the 1910s and continuing for decades. In 1911, Simon Patten, an influential professor of economics at the Wharton School of Business, demanded that schools provide evidence of their contribution to society by showing results that could be "readily seen and measured."[8] Other would-be reformers sought to bring to the school system the fruits of the industrial efficiency movement, founded by Frederick Winslow Taylor, an American engineer who coined the term "scientific management" in 1911.[9] Taylor analyzed the production of pig iron in factories by breaking down the process into its component parts (through time-and-motion studies) and determining standard levels of output for each job. Workers who carried out their tasks more slowly than the prescribed time were paid at a lower rate per unit of output; those who met the expectation were rewarded at a higher rate. Taylor also advocated an elaborate system for monitoring and controlling the workplace.[10] His goal was to increase efficiency by standardizing and speeding up work on the factory floor to create mass production.

Specialization and standardization of tasks, recording and reporting of all activity, pecuniary carrots and sticks—these were the legacy of Taylor and his disciples to subsequent generations.

Taylorism was based on trying to replace the implicit knowledge of the workmen with mass-production methods developed, planned, monitored, and controlled by managers. "Under scientific management," he wrote, "the managers assume ... the burden of gathering together all of the traditional knowledge which in the past has been possessed by the workmen and then of classifying, tabulating, and reducing this knowledge to rules, laws, formulae.... Thus all of the planning which under the old system was done by the workmen, must of necessity under the new system be done by management in accordance with the law of science."[11] According to Taylor, "It is only through *enforced* standardization of methods, *enforced* adoption of the best implements and working conditions, and *enforced* cooperation that this faster work can be assured. And the duty of enforcing the adoption of standards and enforcing this cooperation rests with *management* alone" (italics in original).[12]

Taylorist themes of the need for greater efficiency through standardization and monitoring were reflected in the widely influential textbook *Public School Administration*, published in 1916 by the dean of Stanford University's School of Education, Ellwood P. Cubberley.[13] The notion of judging teachers based on the test scores of their pupils was floated for decades thereafter. One education researcher, William Lancelot, tried to determine the contribution of teachers to their pupils' learning by testing the students' knowledge of mathematics at the beginning and end of the school year to arrive at a "pupil change" score. While some teachers were found to be more effective than others, the gains for pupils who studied with the best teachers were very modest.[14] In the early twenty-first century, the same concept would be revived under the moniker of "value-added scoring" and then, in the Obama years, as "student growth."[15]

Taylorist modes of organizing factory production were increasingly adopted in a wide range of manufacturing industries in the interwar period. By the 1950s they were the norm at companies like General Motors, where, as the sociologist Daniel Bell noted, the managerial "superstructure which organizes and directs production ... draws all possible brainwork away from the shop; everything is centered in the planning and schedule and design departments." The result reinforced the numbing routine for the workers at the bottom of the hierarchy.[16] At the end of the century, metrics would bring these modes of organization out of manufacturing and into the service sector.

MANAGERIALISM AND MEASUREMENT

Taylorism was developed by engineers, but another contribution to the culture of accountability as standardized measurement came from the accounting profession. It was Robert McNamara, an accountant who at the age of 24 became the youngest professor at the Harvard Business School, who carried the message of metrics to the largest organization in the United States: the U.S. Army.

The decades in which McNamara rose from business school professor, to Ford Motor Company executive, to Secretary of Defense, and finally to president of the World Bank also saw the transformation of American business schools. In an earlier era, business schools had focused on preparing their students for jobs in particular industries and enterprises. From the 1950s onward, the business school ideal became the general manager, equipped with a set of skills that were independent of particular industries.

The core of managerial expertise was now defined as a distinct set of skills and techniques, focused upon a mastery of quantitative methodologies.[17] Decisions based on numbers were viewed as scientific, since numbers were thought to imply objectivity and accuracy.[18] Management theorists and gurus who dispensed this new wisdom ascended to the office once ascribed by Shelley to poets as "the unacknowledged legislators of mankind."[19]

Before that, "expertise" meant the career-long accumulation of knowledge of a specific field, as one progressed from rung to rung within the same institution or business—accumulating what economists call "task-specific know-how." Auto executives were "car guys"—men who had spent much of their professional life in the automotive industry. They were increasingly replaced by McNamara-like "bean counters," adept at calculating costs and profit margins.[20]

In time, this attempt to turn management into a science to prepare aspirants for executive positions in corporate America morphed into the gospel of managerialism. The role of judgment grounded in experience and a deep knowledge of context was downplayed. The premise of managerialism is that the differences among organizations—including private corporations, government agencies, and universities—are less important than the similarities. Thus the performance of all organizations can be optimized using the same toolkit of managerial techniques and skills.[21] We might think of judgment and expertise based upon experience as the lubricant that makes organizations flourish by providing task-specific know-how. Managerialism under the spell of metrics tends to ignore, if it does not actually disdain, all that.

As secretary of defense in charge of prosecuting the war in Vietnam, McNamara championed the metric of "body counts" as a purportedly reliable index of American progress in winning the war. Yet few of the generals in the field considered the body count a valid measure of success, and many knew the counts to be exaggerations or outright fabrications.[22] The result, in the pithy formulation of Kenneth Cukier and Viktor Mayer-Schönberger, was a "quagmire of quantification."[23]

McNamara's Pentagon was characterized by what the military strategist Edward Luttwak called "the wholesale substitution of civilian mathematical analysis for military expertise. The new breed of the 'systems analysts' introduced new standards of intellectual discipline and greatly improved book-keeping methods, but also a trained incapacity to understand the most important aspects of military power, which happen to be nonmeasurable."[24] The various armed forces sought to maximize measurable "production": the air force through the number of bombing sorties; artillery through the number of shells fired; infantry through body counts, reflecting statistical indices devised by McNamara and his associates in the Pentagon. But, as Luttwak writes, "In frontless war where there are no clear lines on the map to show victory and defeat, the only true measure of progress must be political and nonquantifiable: the impact on the enemy's will to continue to fight."[25]

Luttwak's critique of the American military establishment, published in 1984, focused on the fact that both its military and civilian leadership had become imbued with a managerial ethos, pursuing measureable "efficiencies" that were at odds with the sort of strategic thinking the military required. "Under the guidance of civilian officials—many of whom care little about their ignorance of strategy, operational craft, and tactics, and present themselves as managers capable of managing all things regardless of their content—the military establishment itself long ago accepted the pursuit of business efficiency as its supreme goal." Military officers were themselves increasingly imbibing a managerial outlook, pursuing degrees in business administration, management, or economics. That led to what Luttwak called a "materialist bias," aimed at measuring inputs and tangible outputs (such as firepower), rather than intangible human factors, such as strategy, leadership, group cohesion, and the morale of servicemen.[26] What could be precisely measured tended to overshadow what was really important. "[W]hile the material inputs are all hard facts, costs precisely stated in dollars and cents, the intangibles are difficult even to define and mostly cannot be measured at all," he noted.[27]

Whether or not Luttwak's characterization was entirely fair, much of what he criticized in the American military establishment was about to transmigrate to a wide range of institutions in the United States and beyond.

One vector of the metric fixation was the rise of management consultants, outfitted with the managerial skills of quantitative analysis, whose first maxim was "If you can't measure it, you can't manage it."[28] Reliance on numbers and quantitative manipulation not only gave the impression of scientific expertise based on "hard" evidence, it also minimized the need for specific, intimate knowledge of the institutions to whom advice was being sold.[29] The culture of management demanded more data—standardized, numerical data.

WHY METRICS BECAME SO POPULAR

As we'll see in our case studies and explore at greater length in the final chapter, there are settings in which metrics, in its various forms, works well. But there are many circumstances in which metric accountability is more dysfunctional than functional, or in which its costs outweigh its benefits. How should we account for the gap between the effectiveness of the culture of measurement, accountability, and transparency, and its ubiquity? Given its many drawbacks, why is it so popular?

While there is no single answer, and no hard proofs, here are some informed guesses.

DISTRUST OF JUDGMENT

The demand for measured accountability and transparency waxes as trust wanes. There is an elective affinity between a democratic society with substantial social mobility and greater ethnic heterogeneity, and the culture of measured accountability. In societies with an established, transgenerational upper class, the members of that class are more likely to feel secure in their positions, to trust one another, and to have imbibed a degree of tacit knowledge about how to govern from their families, giving them a high degree of confidence in their judgments (whether or not that confidence is justified).[1] By contrast, in meritocratic societies with more open and changing elites, those who reach positions of authority are less likely to feel secure in their judgments, and more likely to seek seemingly objective criteria by which to make decisions. And numbers convey the air of objectivity; they imply the exclusion of subjective judgment.[2] Numbers are regarded as "hard," and thus a safer bet for those disposed to doubt their own judgments.

Numerical metrics also give the appearance (if one does not analyze their genesis and relevance too closely) of transparency and objectivity. A good part of their attractiveness is that they appear to be readily understood by all. As the Cambridge literary scholar Stefan Collini has observed, "public debate in modern liberal democracies has come to combine utilitarian valuations with a distrust of procedures that are not mechanically universalizable."[3]

The quest for numerical metrics of accountability is particularly attractive in cultures marked by low social trust. And mistrust of authority has been a leitmotif of American culture since the 1960s. Thus in politics, administration, and many other fields, numbers are valued precisely because they replace reliance on the subjective, experience-based judgments of those in power. The quest for metrics of accountability exerts its spell over those on both the political left and right. There is a close affinity between it and the populist, egalitarian suspicion of authority based on class, expertise, and background.

The demand for greater "accountability," which we saw reflected in the Google Ngram, fed upon the growing distrust of institutions and resentment of authority based on expertise that marked the United States (and to a considerable degree, other Western societies) from the 1960s onward. "Every profession is a conspiracy against the laity," wrote George Bernard Shaw in his play, *The Doctor's Dilemma*. Beginning in the 1970s, what for Shaw had been a *bon mot* increasingly became the operative assumption of public policy. The right and left looked to metrics, though not always for the same reasons.

The suspicion of authority was intrinsic to the post-1960s political left: to rely upon the judgment of experts was to surrender to the prejudices of established elites. Thus, the left had its reasons for advancing an agenda that professed to make institutions accountable and transparent, using the purportedly objective and scientific standards of measured performance.

On the right there was the suspicion, sometimes well founded, that public-sector institutions were being run more for the benefit of their employees than their clients and constituents. In some schools, police departments, and other government agencies, time-serving was indeed a reality, even if not as predominant or universal as its critics alleged. The culture of metric accountability was an understandable attempt to break the stranglehold of entrenched gerontocracy. When institutional establishments came under populist attack, they too resorted to metrics as a means of defense to demonstrate their effectiveness.

In a vicious circle, a lack of social trust leads to the apotheosis of metrics, and faith in metrics contributes to a declining reliance upon judgment. In a series of books, Philip K. Howard has argued that the decline of trust leads to a new mindset in which "[a]voiding human choice in public decisions is not just a theory ... but a kind of theology.... Human choice is considered too dangerous." As a consequence, "Officials no longer are allowed to act on their best judgment"[4] or to exercise discretion, which is judgment about what the particular situation requires.[5] The result is overregulation: an ever tighter web of rules, including the proliferation of rules *within* organizations.[6] Often enough, metrics provides the tools for tightening that web. Over-measurement is a form of overregulation, just as mismeasurement is a form of misregulation.

Another motive for measuring performance is the fear of litigation as a result of the expansion of liability in American tort law. In the course of the twentieth century, earlier doctrinal barriers against suing doctors, hospitals, manufacturers, and municipalities broke down. The expansion of civil rights and environmental law further encouraged litigation.[7] In employment, civil rights laws put new burdens of record-keeping and red tape on private companies as well as government agencies.[8] The result: more and more money is spent on lawyers. And the *perception* of the United States as a litigious society[9] creates an anxiety about the possibility of being sued, leading to defensiveness and risk-aversion. The urge to document every decision in the most objective way possible, so that hiring and promotion decisions can be made transparent to regulatory authorities, or used in case of litigation, provides another motivation for measuring performance.

THE CRITIQUE OF THE PROFESSIONS AND THE APOTHEOSIS OF CHOICE

On the political right, the mistrust of public-sector institutions led to the oft-stated conviction that the problem with the nonprofit sectors (government, schools, universities) is that they have "no bottom line" and hence no way of accounting for success or failure. To this way of thinking, the solution is to create a substitute bottom line in the form of "objective"—and preferably numerical—measures of standardized processes.

A parallel trend came from advocates of women's health and later movements that challenged established institutions (such as physicians) and sought to make them more responsive. They looked to give patients greater control over their medical care. That entailed giving them a greater choice of providers, and more information—including performance metrics—to inform those choices. The road to empowerment was paved with metrics.

In one field after another, the introduction of greater measurement in the name of accountability did shine light upon real problems, including variations in professional practice that were supposedly grounded in "science," and gaps in performance that had previously gone unnoticed or undocumented. The impact of these revelations both diminished faith in professional judgment and created pressure to find solutions, solutions thought to entail greater measurement in order to monitor the professionals whose ethos had been cast into doubt.

Closely related to these trends was the rising influence of the ideology of consumer choice, the belief that once provided with information, people will make the right choice when it comes to medical care, education, retirement planning, and so forth. Often, indeed, individuals *are* most capable of deciding on the best provider of services. But not always, and in some domains choice is particularly fraught. In healthcare, for example, choices pertaining to physicians or hospitals are made either when patients are healthy and disinclined to bother with medical matters, or when they are sick and therefore more anxious about their decisions, which diminishes their ability to process complex and often conflicting metrics. Yet by the 1990s, despite a number of studies indicating that patient empowerment did nothing to contain costs or improve quality of care, the model of the patient as consumer in the marketplace of medical services became ever more popular among politicians and policymakers on both sides of the political spectrum.[10]

THE COST DISEASE

Another impetus for accountability in the fields of medicine and education stems from the fact that the relative cost of these services has risen compared to the costs of most consumer goods. Part of the reason lies in "the cost disease," a phenomenon first identified by the economists William Baumol and William Bowen in 1966. They observed that the past hundred years had seen steady increases in productivity in manufacturing, largely the product of improved technology.[11] As technological developments and the intensification of global trade has led to ever-declining costs of most consumer goods, the relatively higher costs of medicine, education, and similar human services have become ever more salient—and a focus of increasing public discontent. Over the years, these trends have led to public pressure for greater efficiency and greater accountability—despite the difficulty of measuring inputs, outputs, and hence productivity in these fields.[12] Add to this the fact that improvements in medical technology and more effective pharmaceuticals may legitimately add to costs: their added costs may well be worth it if people live longer or more pleasant lives and need to spend less time in the hospital.

LEADERSHIP AMID ORGANIZATIONAL COMPLEXITY

Other economic forces are also at play in the push for quantifiable measurements. As organizations (companies, universities, government agencies) become larger and more diversified, there is an ever greater remove between top management and those further down the organizational chain engaged in the actual activities to which the organization is dedicated. When institutions are particularly large, complex, and made up of dissimilar parts, that comprehension is simply impossible. Those at the top face to a greater degree than most of us a cognitive constraint that confronts all of us: making decisions despite having limited time and ability to deal with information overload. Metrics are a tempting means of dealing with this "bounded rationality," and engaging with matters beyond one's comprehension.

Imagine, for example, that you become the president of a large university, corporation, or cabinet department. You might, of course, rely on the informed opinion of experienced subordinates. But they are likely to have an intrinsic interest in the status quo: recall the dictum of the late poet and historian Robert Conquest—"Everyone is conservative about what they know best." But what if you want to inject dynamism or change into an organization whose leadership you have just assumed (and this is the typical temptation of new cabinet secretaries, university presidents, and CEOs who long to "make a mark")? Then getting your hands on "the numbers" seems like the most direct shortcut to comprehending your organization.

The problem is that management's quest to get a handle on a complex organization often leads to what Yves Morieux and Peter Tollman have dubbed "complicatedness": the expansion of procedures for reporting and decision-making, requiring ever more coordination bodies, meetings, and report-writing. With all that time spent reporting, meeting, and coordinating, there is little time left for actual *doing*.[13]

This drain on time and effort is exacerbated by the tendency of executives under the spell of metric fixation to distrust the experienced judgment of those under them. They are more willing to try to control subordinates through a variety of strategies, of which metrics is a central component. The demands for a constant stream of reports and standardized data have the effect, intended or inadvertent, of diminishing the autonomy of those lower in the organizational hierarchy—whose doubts about metrics-based innovations are dismissed as irrational or as a self-interested "resistance to change."

Then there are the cultural peculiarities of some American bureaucracies (corporate, governmental, and nonprofit), which assume that each person can and should be rotated through an ascending hierarchy of posts, both within an organization and among organizations. This militates against developing a depth of expertise that would allow for meaningful evaluation of the significance and qualitative importance of work done by subordinates. Hence the attractiveness of relying on measurable, quantitative, criteria.

CEOs, university presidents, and heads of government agencies move from one organization to another to a greater degree now than in the past. A strange, egalitarian alchemy often assumes that there must be someone better to be found *outside* the organization than within it: that no one within the organization is good enough to ascend, but unknown people from other places might be.[14] That assumption leads to a turnover of top leaders, executives, and managers, who arrive at their new posts with limited substantive knowledge of the institutions they are to manage. Hence their greater reliance on metrics, and preferably metrics that are similar from one organization to another (aka "best practices"). These outsiders-turned-insiders, lacking the deep knowledge of context that comes from experience, are more dependent on standardized forms of measurement. Not only that, but with an eye on their eventual exit to some better job with another organization, mobile managers are on the lookout for metrics of performance that can be deployed when the headhunter calls.

THE LURE OF IT

Yet another factor is the spread of information technology (IT). In the early 1980s the invention and rapid adoption of the electronic spreadsheet and the resulting ease of tabulating and manipulating figures had wide-ranging effects. As a prescient analyst of the phenomenon, Steven Levy, wrote in 1984,

> The spreadsheet is a tool, but it is also a worldview—reality by the numbers.... Because spreadsheets can do so many important things, those who use them tend to lose sight of the crucial fact that the imaginary businesses that they can create on their computers are just that—imaginary. You can't really duplicate a business inside a computer, just aspects of a business. And since numbers are the strength of spreadsheets, the aspects that get emphasized are the ones easily embodied in numbers. Intangible factors aren't so easily quantified.[15]

Seth Klarman, among the most successful value investors of his generation, concurred, warning in 1991 that spreadsheets created the illusion of depth of analysis.[16]

Since then, the growing opportunities to collect data, and the declining cost of doing so, contribute to the meme that data is the answer, for which organizations have to come up with the questions. There is an often unexamined faith that amassing data and sharing it widely within the organization will result in improvements of some sort—even if much information has to be denuded of nuance and context to turn it into easily transferred "data."

PRINCIPALS, AGENTS, AND MOTIVATION

During the same decades that professional expertise was coming under fire, the business corporation also came in for critique as favoring the interests of its managers over those of its shareholders.

The notion picked up steam in the 1970s and achieved a kind of academic quintessence in "principal-agent theory."[1] The version of the theory prominent in the management literature calls attention to the gap between the purposes of institutions and the people who run them and are employed by them. It focuses on the problem of aligning the interests of shareholders in maximum profitability and stock price with the interests of corporate executives, whose priorities might diverge from those goals. Principal-agent theory articulates in abstract terms the general suspicion that those employed in institutions are not to be trusted; that their activity must be monitored and measured; that those measures need to be transparent to those without firsthand knowledge of the institutions; and that pecuniary rewards and punishments are the most effective way to motivate "agents."[2] Here too, numbers are seen as a guarantee of objectivity, and as a replacement for intimate knowledge and personal trust.[3]

Principal-agent theory led at first to schemes to remunerate CEOs with bonuses based on the profits and stock price of the companies they headed. Later, it morphed into plans to provide top managers with stock options of their companies. The idea in each case was to align the incentives of the managers with those of the owners of the firm, whose sole interest was presumed, quite plausibly, to be the profitability of the company.

Principal-agent theory conceives of organizations as networks of relationships between those with a given interest (the principals) and those hired to carry out that interest (the agents). The perspective is that of the principals, and the premise is that the interests of the agents may diverge from those of the principals. The interests of the shareholders of a company, for example, may be to maximize profits and returns on their capital. But the interests of their managers might be to have ostentatious offices and conspicuous private planes that raise their status, and the interests of lower-level employees might be to claim a salary while minimizing their workload. The challenge for the principal is to incentivize the agents to carry out his priorities, rather than their own priorities. A corollary problem for the principal is that of monitoring: how can he know what his agents are actually doing, and how well they are carrying out his goals? The twin tasks of organizations thus becomes how to provide information to organizational superiors about the activities of their subordinates, and how to create systems of reward to align the interests of the agents with those of the principals. The quest for information leads to performance metrics: standardized numbers that will efficiently convey to the principals how well their agents are carrying out the principals' goals. Aligning incentives is taken to mean giving monetary rewards to employees that reflect the profitability of the firm: when the firm makes more money, so do the employees.

The professional management literature derived its own conclusions from principal-agent theory: that management is a matter of setting clear goals, and then of monitoring and incentivizing. It relies upon information and reporting systems on the one hand, and cleverly structured rewards on the other.

NEW PUBLIC MANAGEMENT

Beginning in the 1980s, this sort of thinking was extended from profit-making corporations to government agencies and such nonprofit organizations as universities and hospitals. Discontent with the costs, dissatisfaction with outcomes, or simply the desire to save money led critics to argue that the problem with these organizations was that they needed to function "more like a business." That was the battle-cry of advocates of what became known as the "New Public Management." The principals were in the first instance those who paid for agencies and nonprofit organizations: in the case of government, the taxpayers. The organizations' students, patients, or clients were now to be regarded as their customers.

One difficulty, for those who sought to make such organizations more like a business, was that there was no price mechanism by which to determine whether those who supplied the funds were getting good value for their money. In a competitive market, consumers can compare the price of goods and services with the quality of the products on offer, and can make informed decisions about what to buy. Prices convey a lot of information in a concise, transparent form. But how were the taxpayers to evaluate schools, universities, hospitals, government agencies, or charitable organizations? To resolve these difficulties, those who sought to make nonprofit organizations more businesslike suggested three strategies. The first was to try to develop indicators that would measure performance and would serve as a replacement for price.[4] The second was to offer monetary rewards and punishments, based on measured performance, to those who worked in these organizations. The third was to provide competition among providers whose performance indicators would be "transparent," that is, publicly available. The idea, in short, was to create marketlike conditions within the government and nonprofit sectors; and thus to run them "more like a business." That was the way of thinking dubbed the "new public management." It reflected a broader trend of importing principles from microeconomics into public administration and public policy.[5]

From the beginning, there were critics who tried to draw attention to the flawed premises of this approach, such as the economists Bengt Holmström and Paul Milgrom, as well as Henry Mintzberg, a professor of management at McGill University in Montreal.[6] Mintzberg pointed out in the mid-1990s that the conception of management adopted by advocates of the New Public Management was a simplified caricature of what effective managers in private-sector firms actually did. It did conform, though, to what many students of management were being taught in business schools and in the burgeoning literature of business advice. Even then, it was inappropriate for government and nonprofit organizations, he argued. Business corporations have divisions where each unit has a clear mission to deliver a particular set of products or services; but government agencies and nonprofit organizations are characterized by multiple purposes, which are difficult to isolate and to measure. New Public Management schemes are plausible solutions for dealing with units of government that produce a single product or service, such as issuing passports. But that is the exception rather than the rule. Moreover, in business there are clear financial criteria of success and failure: costs and benefits can be compared to determine profits, and managers can plausibly be rewarded on that basis. But in government and nonprofit organizations there are rarely single goals, and they cannot be readily measured. Primary schools, for example, have their tasks of teaching reading, writing, and numeracy, and these perhaps could be monitored through standardized tests. But what about goals that are less measureable but no less important, such as instilling good behavior, inspiring a curiosity about the world, and fostering creative thought?

There is a larger problem. Firms are in the business of making profits, and their employees work at their jobs primarily to make money. (Which does not mean that money is their ultimate goal, only that they work in large part to earn money to use for their own, nonmonetary purposes.) People who choose to work for government agencies and nonprofit organizations, such as schools, universities, hospitals, or the Red Cross, are also interested in earning a living, but they tend to be more motivated by a commitment to the mission of the organization: to teach, to research, to heal, to rescue. They respond differently to the lure of monetary rewards, because their motivations are different, at least in degree.[7]

EXTRINSIC AND INTRINSIC REWARDS

Many of the problems of pay-for-performance schemes can be traced to an overly simple, indeed deeply distortive, conception of human motivation, one that assumes that people are motivated to work only by material rewards. For some are motivated less by *extrinsic* monetary rewards than by various sorts of *intrinsic* psychic rewards, including their commitment to the goals of the organizations for which they work, or a fascination with the complexity of the work they do, which makes it challenging, interesting, and entertaining. The existence of intrinsic as well as extrinsic motivations is obvious to anyone who has managed workers in complex tasks. It was articulated in the mid-1970s by psychologists, and has since been rediscovered and formalized by economists, including Jean Tirole, a recent recipient of the Nobel Prize for economics.[8]

It is simple-minded to assume that people are motivated only by the desire for more money, and naive to assume that they are motivated only by intrinsic rewards. The challenge is to figure out when each of these motivations is most effective, and in recent years social scientists have devoted attention to that issue.

In general, extrinsic rewards—pay-for-performance, incentive pay, bonuses—are most effective in commercial organizations, where the primary goal is to make money. They also work well when the task to be completed is discrete, easily measured, and not of much intrinsic interest, such as the production of some standardized good on an assembly line.

Some rewards enhance intrinsic motivation. For example, when the rewards are verbal and expressed primarily to convey information ("You did a great job on that!") rather than to exercise control.[9] Or when awards are given out after the fact, for excellence in achievement, without having been offered as an incentive in advance.[10] Or, in fields such as science or scholarship, when prizes or honorific titles are bestowed to recognize long-term achievement.[11] More broadly, above-market wages can reinforce employees' intrinsic motivation if those wages are perceived as a *signal* of the organization's *appreciation* of the employees' performance.[12] Intrinsic and extrinsic motivation can work in tandem when the outcomes that are rewarded are in keeping with the agents' own sense of mission: when hospitals, for example, are rewarded for better safety records.

But when mission-oriented organizations try to use extrinsic rewards, as in promises of pay-for-performance, the result may actually be counterproductive. The use of extrinsic rewards for activities of high intrinsic interest leads people to focus on the rewards and not on the intrinsic interest of the task, or on the larger mission of which it is a part. The result is a "crowding out" of intrinsic motivation: having been taught to think of their work tasks primarily as a means toward monetary goals, they lose interest in doing the work for the sake of the larger mission of the institution.[13] Alternatively, they may perceive the offer of payment for performance as an insult to their professional ethics, and indeed to their self-esteem, implying that they are in it for the money. Therefore, the assumption that extrinsic rewards encourage performance makes a lot of sense if one is an investment banker, but not if one is a teacher or nurse. Trying to turn everything into a business, then, gets in the way of the actual business at hand.

Indeed, it impedes actual businesses. Ironically, even as corporations were falling over one another to develop incentive schemes based on pay for measured performance for their top executives and employees, and such schemes were being touted as appropriate for the government and nonprofit organizations, top theorists of principal-agent behavior by the end of the twentieth century were exploring the weaknesses of such systems. By 1998, Robert Gibbons, a professor of organizational economics at MIT, pointed out that in fact the principal (the owner of the firm, for example) profits from a *variety* of outputs from the agent (the employee), and that many of these outputs are not highly visible or measureable in any numerical sense. Organizations depend on employees engaging in mentoring and in team work, for example, which are often at odds with what the employees would do if their only interests were to maximize their measured performance for purposes of compensation. Thus, there is a gap between the *measureable* contribution and the *actual*, total contribution of the agent. As a result, measured performance (such as an increase in the division's profits or a rise in the company's stock price) may actually lead to the organization getting less of what it really needs from its employees. Moreover, there was an inevitable distortion of incentives created by the quest for simple, quantifiable standards by which to measure and reward performance. Gibbons concluded that at best, economic models that ignore the range of psychological motives for why agents derive reward from working provide a truncated conception of motives. At worst, "management practices based on economic models may dampen (or even destroy) noneconomic realities such as intrinsic motivation and social relations."[14]

By the end of the twentieth century, students of organizational behavior like Gibbons were calling attention to the pitfalls of appeals to extrinsic motivation. But by then, schemes based upon simple conceptions of incentives, extrinsic reward, and New Public Management were already well entrenched.

These managerial fashions began in the corporate sector but quickly spread beyond it, above all in the Anglosphere (Great Britain, the United States, Australia, and New Zealand). To try to improve the management and efficiency of the public sector, the Conservative government of Margaret Thatcher established official bodies, some staffed by businessmen and management consultants, with titles such as the Efficiency

Unit, the Financial Management Unit, the National Audit Office, and the Audit Commission. From Britain, the fashion spread to Australia and New Zealand, and to other OECD countries, carried beyond national borders by management gurus, consultants, and academics peddling tools and models of "best practice."[15]

PHILOSOPHICAL CRITIQUES

Just as the culture of metrics has its boosters on both the political right and left, it also has critics from both sides of the ideological spectrum. From the perspective of the Marxist left, it can be seen, with some justification, as promoting deskilling, in which changes in the organization of production brought about by those at the top have the effect of devaluing the skills and experience of those subordinate in the system.[1] And work that is more circumscribed, and from which discretion has been excised by having to meet narrowly defined goals dictated by others, is more alienating.

THE RATIONALIST ILLUSION

There are also powerful dissections of accountability-as-measurement from conservative and classical liberal thinkers, such as Michael Oakeshott, Michael Polanyi, and Friedrich Hayek, whose analysis has recently been rediscovered by James C. Scott, a Yale anthropologist with self-described anarchist predilections. They have all distinguished between two forms of knowledge, one abstract and formulaic, the other more practical and tacit. Practical or tacit knowledge is the product of experience: it can be learned, but cannot be conveyed in general formulas. Abstract knowledge, by contrast, is a matter of technique, which, it is assumed, can be easily systematized, conveyed, and applied. In Oakeshott's famous example, there is the sort of abstract, recipe knowledge conveyed by cookbooks; but actually knowing how to make use of such knowledge ("beat an egg," "whisk the mixture") requires practical knowledge, based upon experience, that cannot be learned from books. Oakeshott criticized "rationalists" for assuming that the conduct of human affairs is a matter of applying the right formulas or recipes. Technical knowledge is susceptible to precise formulation, which gives it the appearance of certainty. By contrast, he wrote,

> [I]t is a characteristic of practical knowledge that it is not susceptible of formulation of this kind. Its normal expression is in a customary or traditional way of doing things, or, simply, in practice. And this gives it the appearance of imprecision and consequently of uncertainty, of being a matter of opinion, of probability rather than truth.

The rationalist believes in the sovereignty of technique in which the only form of authentic knowledge is technical knowledge, for it alone satisfies the standard of certainty that marks *real* knowledge. The error of rationalism, for Oakeshott, is its failure to appreciate the necessity of practical knowledge and of knowledge of the peculiarity of circumstances.[2]

SCIENTISM

Friedrich Hayek developed a related critique of what he called "the pretense of knowledge." Writing in the mid-twentieth century, he chastised socialist attempts at large-scale economic planning for their "scientism," by which he meant their attempt to engineer economic life, as if planners were in a position to know all the relevant inputs and outputs that make up life in a complex society. The advantage of the competitive market, he maintained, is that it allows individuals not only to make use of their knowledge of local conditions, but to discover new uses for existing resources or imagine new products and services hitherto unknown and unsuspected. In short, planning failed not only to consider relevant but dispersed information, but it also prohibited the entrepreneurial discovery of how to meet particular needs and how to generate new goals.[3]

Ironically, as a number of contemporary critics have observed, the fixation on quantifiable goals so central to metric fixation—though often implemented by politicians and policymakers who proclaim their devotion to capitalism—replicates many of the intrinsic faults of the Soviet system. Just as Soviet bloc planners set output targets for each factory to produce, so do bureaucrats set measurable performance targets for schools, hospitals, police forces, and corporations. And just as Soviet managers responded by producing shoddy goods that met the numerical targets set by their overlords, so do schools, police forces, and businesses find ways of fulfilling quotas with shoddy goods of their own: by graduating pupils with minimal skills, or downgrading grand theft to misdemeanor-level petty larceny, or opening dummy accounts for bank clients.[4]

A good deal of Hayek's critique of scientism (which he also applied to much of modern economics) also pertains to the ideology of metrics. By setting out in advance a limited and purportedly measurable set of goals, metric fixation truncates the range of actual goals of a business or organization. It also precludes entrepreneurship within organizations, as there may be new goals and purposes worth pursuing that are not part of the metric.

One could draw together the insights of a number of thinkers into this dictum: The calculative is the enemy of the imaginative. Entrepreneurship, as we have noted, depends on taking what the economist Frank Knight termed "unmeasureable risk," for the potential benefits of an innovation are not subject to precise calculation. Or in the formulation of Alfie Kohn, a long-time critic of pay-for-performance, metrics "inhibits risk-taking, an inevitable concomitant of exploration and creativity. We are less likely to take chances, to play with possibilities, and to follow hunches, which may, after all, not pay off."[5]

A hallmark of practical, local knowledge, as James Scott has noted, is that "it is as economical and accurate as it needs to be, no more and no less, for addressing the problem at hand."[6] By contrast, the degree of numerical precision promised by metrics may be far greater than is required by actual practitioners, and attaining that precision requires an expenditure of time and effort that may not be worthwhile. The quest for precision may therefore be wasteful, and resented for that reason by those required to sacrifice their time and ingenuity.

"To demand or preach mechanical precision, even in principle, in a field incapable of it is to be blind and to mislead others," as the British liberal philosopher Isaiah Berlin noted in an essay on political judgment. Indeed what Berlin says of political judgment applies more broadly: judgment is a sort of skill at grasping the unique particularities of a situation, and it entails a talent for synthesis rather than analysis, "a capacity for taking in the total pattern of a human situation, of the way in which things hang together."[7] A feel for the whole and a sense for the unique are precisely what numerical metrics cannot supply.

KEDOURIE'S CRITIQUE OF THATCHER

In 1987 the Conservative government of Margaret Thatcher developed wide-ranging plans for transforming the public funding of higher education. The plan called for a plethora of new "performance indicators," on the evidence of which ministers and their bureaucracies were to decide upon the allocation of funds to particular universities. The distinguished British conservative historian and political theorist Elie Kedourie emerged as one of the plan's most scathing critics. "After two decades of government-sponsored excess and prodigality," he wrote, "we see now abroad a vague but powerful discontent and impatience with the ways of universities . . . a nameless yearning for some formula or recipe— more science perhaps, more information technology, more questionnaires, more monitoring—which will scientifically (or better, magically) prove that they are not wasting their time, which will hook them up with the humming conveyorbelts of industry."[8] He wondered in astonishment that "a Conservative administration should have embarked on a university policy so much at variance with its proclaimed ideals and objectives," and concluded that "[i]n order to explain the inexplicable, one is driven to conclude that the policy is an outcome not of conscious decisions, but of an unconscious automatic response to an irresistible spirit of the times."[9] Under the slogan of "efficiency" a great fraud was being perpetrated, Kedourie declared, for "efficiency is not a general and abstract attribute. It is always relative to the object in view. A business is more efficient when its return on the factors employed in production is greater than that of another, comparable one. But a university is not a business."[10] Under the pretense that it was a business, and that the government represented its customers, Kedourie observed that it was the Minister of Education who would decide, on the basis of spurious criteria, what constituted educational value.[11]

THE ONWARD MARCH OF ACCOUNTABILITY

In the decade that followed, "accountability" and "performance measurement" became buzzwords among business leaders, politicians, and policymakers in the United States as well. In 1993, President Bill Clinton signed the Government Performance and Results Act, which required all agencies to develop mission statements, long-range strategic plans, and annual performance goals, together with descriptions of the measures to be used to gauge progress toward those goals. Initiated by Republican legislators and signed by a Democratic president, the act enjoyed bipartisan support.[12] In 2004, during the presidency of George W. Bush, the federal government's venerable General Accounting Office was rechristened the Government Accountability Office.

With that we enter our own age, and move from the history and theory of measured performance to its contemporary practice.

THE MISMEASURE OF
ALL THINGS?

CASE STUDIES

COLLEGES AND UNIVERSITIES

Let's take as our first case study the realm of higher education, the ground zero of my own investigations of metric fixation. Comprising a huge sector of the national economy and a central institution of all advanced societies, colleges and universities exemplify many of the characteristic flaws and unintended consequences of measured performance, as well as some of its advantages.

RAISING THE METRIC: EVERYONE SHOULD GO TO COLLEGE

Once we become fixated on measurement, we easily slip into believing that more is better.

More and more Americans are going on to post–high school education, encouraged to do so by both governments and nonprofit organizations. According to the U.S. Department of Education, for example, "In today's world, college is not a luxury that only some Americans can afford to enjoy; it is an economic, civic, and personal necessity for *all* Americans."[1]

One of many nonprofit organizations that convey the same message is the Lumina Foundation. Its mission is to expand post-secondary educational attainment, with a goal of having 60 percent of Americans hold a college degree, certificate, or other "high-quality postsecondary credential" by the year 2025. Its "Stronger Nation" initiative, as the foundation declares on its website, is all about the evidence of that learning—quantifying it, tracking it, pinpointing the places where it is and isn't happening. . . . Lumina is also working with state policy leaders across the nation to set attainment goals and develop and implement strong state plans to reach them. So far, 26 states have set rigorous and challenging attainment goals—15 in the last year alone. Most of these states are taking concrete steps—such as implementing outcomes-based funding, improving developmental education, and making higher education more affordable—to increase attainment and reach their goals.[2]

The Lumina Foundation is steeped in metrics and proselytizes on its behalf: its website proclaims, "As an organization focused on results, Lumina Foundation uses a set of national metrics to guide our work, measure our impact and monitor the nation's progress toward Goal 2025."

The Lumina Foundation's mission comports with a widely shared conviction about the role of higher education in American society: the belief that ever more people should go on to college, and that doing so increases not only their own lifetime earnings but also creates national economic growth.

RAISING THE NUMBER OF WINNERS LOWERS THE VALUE OF WINNING

That article of faith, and the performance targets to which it gives rise, may simply be mistaken. As Alison Wolf, an educational economist at the University of London, has pointed out, it is true that those who have a B.A. tend to earn more on average than those without one. Thus, on the individual level, the quest for a B.A. degree may make economic sense. But on the national level, the idea that more university graduates means higher productivity is a fallacy.[3]

One reason for that is that to a large extent education is a positional good—at least when it comes to the job market. For potential employers, degrees act as signals: they serve as a shorthand that allows employers to rank initial applicants for a job. Having completed high school signals a certain, modest level of intellectual competence as well as personality traits such as persistence. Finishing college is a signal of a somewhat higher level of each of these. In a society where a small minority successfully completes college, having a B.A. signals a certain measure of superiority. But the higher the percentage of people with a B.A., the lower its value as a sorting device. What happens instead is that jobs that once required only a high school diploma now require a B.A. That is not because the jobs have become more cognitively demanding or require a higher level of skill, but because employers can afford to choose from among the many applicants who hold a B.A., while excluding the rest. The result is both to depress the wages of those who lack a college degree, and to place many college graduates in jobs that don't actually make use of the substance of their college education.[4] That leads to a positional arms race: as word spreads that a college diploma is the entry ticket to even modest jobs, more and more people seek degrees.

Thus, there are private incentives for increasing numbers of people to try to obtain a college degree. Meanwhile, governments and private organizations set performance measures aimed at raising college attendance and graduation.

HIGHER METRICS THROUGH LOWER STANDARDS

But the fact that more Americans are entering college does not mean that they are prepared to do so, or that all Americans are capable of actually earning a meaningful college degree.

In fact, there is no indication that more students are leaving high school prepared for college-level work.[5] One measure of college preparedness is the performance of students on achievement tests, such as the SAT and the ACT, which are used to predict likely success in college (they are, in part, aptitude tests). For the most part, these tests are taken only by high school students who have some hope of going on to higher education, though in an effort to boost student achievement, some states have taken to mandating that ever more students take such tests. (Probably a case of misplaced causation. Students who took the tests tended to have higher levels of achievement. So, it was mistakenly reasoned, by getting more students to take the test, levels of achievement would be raised. The flaw is that better-performing students were more likely to take the test in the first place. That is, policymakers mistook cause for effect.) The ACT tests four subject areas: English, math, reading, and science. The company that develops the ACT has developed benchmarks of scores that indicate that the test taker has a "strong readiness for college course work." Of those who took the ACT test most recently, a third did not meet the benchmark in *any* of the four categories, and only 38 percent met the benchmarks in at least three of the four areas. In short, most of those who aspire to go on to college do not have the demonstrated ability to do so.[6]

The results are predictable—though few want to acknowledge them. Since more students enter community colleges and four-year colleges inadequately prepared, a large portion require remedial courses. These are courses (now euphemistically rechristened "developmental" courses) that cover what the student ought to have learned in high school. A third of students who enter community colleges are placed in developmental reading classes, and more than 59 percent are placed in developmental mathematics courses.[7] Students who are inadequately prepared for college also make additional demands on the institutions they attend, thus raising the costs of college education: the growth on campuses of centers of "educational excellence" is a euphemistic response to the need for more extracurricular help in writing and other skills for students inadequately prepared for university-level work.

Colleges, both public and private, are measured and rewarded based in part on their graduation rates, which are one of the criteria by which colleges are ranked, and in some cases, remunerated. (Recall the Lumina Foundation's encouragement of state governments to engage in "outcomes-based funding.") What then happens is that outcomes follow funding. By allowing more students to pass, a college transparently demonstrates its accountability through its excellent metric of performance. What is not so transparent is the lowered standards demanded for graduation.[8] More courses are offered with requirements that are easily fulfilled. There is pressure on professors—sometimes overt, sometimes tacit[9]—to be generous in awarding grades. An ever-larger portion of the teaching faculty comprises adjunct instructors—and an adjunct who fails a substantial portion of her class (even if their performance merits it) is less likely to have her contract renewed.

Thus, more students are entering colleges and universities. A consequence of students entering college without the ability to do college-level work is the ever larger number of students who enroll but do not complete their degrees—a widespread and growing phenomenon that has substantial costs for the students who do so, in tuition, living expenses, and earnings foregone.[10] High dropout rates seem to indicate that too many students are attempting college, not too few.[11] And those who *do* obtain degrees find that a generic B.A. is of diminishing economic value, because it signals less and less to potential employers about real ability and achievement.[12]

Recognizing this, prospective college students and their parents seek admission not just to any college, but to a highly ranked one.[13] And that, in turn, has led to the arms race of college rankings, a topic to which we will return.

Lowering the standards for obtaining a B.A. means that using the percentage of those who attain a college degree as an indicator of "human capital" becomes a deceptive unit of measurement for public policy analysis. Economists can evaluate only what they can measure, and what they can measure needs to be standardized. Thus economists who work on "human capital" and its contribution to economic growth (and who almost always conclude that what the economy needs is more college graduates) often use college graduation rates as their measure of "human capital" attainment, ignoring the fact that not all B.A.'s are the same, and that some may not reflect much ability or achievement. This lends a certain air of unreality to the explorations of what one might call the unworldly economists, who combine hard measures of statistical validity with weak interest in the validity of the units of measurement.

One assumption that lies behind the effort to boost levels of college enrollment and completion is that increases in average educational attainment somehow translate into higher levels of national economic growth. But some distinguished economists on both sides of the Atlantic—Alison Wolf in England, and Daron Acemoglu and David Autor in the United States—have concluded that that is no longer the case, if it ever was. In an age in which technology is replacing many tasks previously performed by those with low to moderate levels of human capital, national economic growth based on innovation and technological progress depends not so much on the average level of educational attainment as on the attainment of those at the top of the distribution of knowledge, ability, and skill.[14] In recent decades, the percentage of the population with a college degree has gone up, while the rate of economic growth has declined. And though the gap between the earnings of those with and those without a college diploma remains substantial, the falling rate of earnings for college graduates seems to indicate that the economy already has an oversupply of graduates.[15] By contrast, there is a shortage of workers in the skilled trades, such as plumbers, carpenters, and electricians— occupations in which training occurs through apprenticeship rather than through college education—who often earn more than those with four-year degrees.[16]

To be sure, public policy ought to aim at more than economic growth, and there is more to college education than its effect on earning capacity, as we will explore in a moment. But for now, it is worth underscoring that the metric goal of ever more college graduates is dubious even by the economistic criteria by which higher education is often measured.

PRESSURE TO MEASURE COLLEGE PERFORMANCE

In the decades since Elie Kedourie penned his critique of the centralizing policy of Margaret Thatcher's Conservative government, central government control over British institutions of higher education has expanded and intensified. Much of that control takes the form of management through performance metrics. For scholarship in many fields, the results have been deleterious.

In England, as elsewhere, an ever larger proportion of the population is attending university, in keeping with the government's aims. In 1970 less than 10 percent of men and women in each age cohort attended university. By 1997, it was close to a third, and by 2012, 38 percent of nineteen-year-olds were enrolled in some form of tertiary education.[17] Paying for them is an ever more onerous task, and in recent years the costs have been increasingly shifted to the students themselves (or their families) in the form of tuition fees. But government expenditure remains substantial, and in an effort to control expenses and achieve "value," that control increasingly takes the form of payment for purported results. That performance is evaluated through metrics that focus upon the measured output of each department and institution.

In an attempt to obtain "value," successive British administrations have created a series of government agencies charged with evaluating the country's universities, with titles such as the "Quality Assurance Agency."[18] There are audits of teaching quality, such as the "Teaching Quality Assessment," evaluated largely on the extent to which various procedures are followed and paperwork filed, few of which have much to do with actual teaching.[19] But one clear result has been that professors are forced to devote more and more of their time to paperwork rather than to research or teaching. And there has been a ballooning of the number of professional staff, including the newly created post of "quality assurance officers," dedicated to gathering and analyzing the data for what was once known as the Research Assessment Exercise, since rechristened as the Research Excellence Framework.[20] The cost of these exercises in metrics in England alone was estimated at £250,000,000 in 2002.[21] A mushroom-like growth of administrative staff has occurred in other countries that have adopted similar systems of performance measurement, such as Australia. In most such systems, metrics has diverted time and resources away from doing and toward documenting, and from those who teach and research to those who gather and disseminate the data for the Research Assessment Exercise and its counterparts.[22] The search for more data means more data managers, more bureaucracy, more expensive software systems. Ironically, in the name of controlling costs, expenditures wax.

The closest parallel in the United States are the accrediting organizations that grant legitimacy to American colleges and universities. They are regional in scope, but since receiving federal funds requires accreditation by such agencies, they also serve as instruments of the federal government.[23] While they do not control funding in the manner of their British counterparts, they play a major role nevertheless. And in recent decades, that role has been to pressure the colleges and universities they accredit to adopt ever more elaborate measures of performance, under the rubric of "assessment."[24]

Reward for measured performance in higher education is touted by its boosters as making universities "more like a business." But businesses have a built-in restraint on devoting too much time and money to measurement—at some point, it cuts into profits. Ironically, since universities and other nonprofit institutions have no such bottom line, government or accrediting agencies or the university's administrative leadership can extend metrics endlessly.[25] The effect is to increase costs or to divert spending from the doers to the administrators—which usually suits the latter just fine. It is hard to find a university where the ratio of administrators to professors and of administrators to students has not risen astronomically in recent decades.[26] And the same holds true on the national level.

THE RANKING ARMS RACE

Another increasingly influential set of performance metrics in the field of higher education are university rankings. They take a variety of forms. On the international level, there is the Shanghai Jiao Tong "Academic Ranking of World Universities" (which was developed to provide the Chinese government a "global benchmark" against which Chinese universities could assess their progress in an attempt to catch up on "hard scientific research" and hence gives a 90 percent weighting to publications and awards in the natural sciences and mathematics)[27] and the *Times Higher Education Supplement* "World University Rankings," which tries to include teaching, research (including volume of publications and citations), and "international outlook." Within the United States, the most influential ratings are those of *US News and World Report* (*USNWR*), with competition from *Forbes, Newsweek, Princeton Review, Kiplinger* (which tries to balance quality with affordability), and a host of others. These rankings (or "league tables" as they are known in Britain) are an important source of prestige: alumni and members of the board of trustees are anxious to have their institutions rate highly, as are potential donors and, of course, potential students. Maintaining or improving the institution's rankings tends to become a priority for university presidents and their top administrators.[28] Indeed, some American university presidents are awarded contracts that specify a bonus if they are able to raise the school's rank. So are other top administrators: since one factor that affects rankings is the achievement scores of incoming students, the dean of admissions of at least one law school was remunerated based in part on the scores of the admitted students.[29]

Recently I was puzzled to find that a mid-ranked American university was taking out full-page advertisements in every issue of *The Chronicle of Higher Education,* touting the important issues on which its faculty members were working. Since the *Chronicle* is read mostly by academics—and especially academic administrators—I scratched my head at the tremendous expenditures of this not particularly rich university on a seemingly superfluous ad campaign. Then it struck me: the *USNWR* ratings are based in good part on surveys of college presidents, asking them to rank the prestige of other universities. The criterion is of dubious validity, since most presidents are simply unaware of developments at most other institutions. The ad campaign was aimed at raising awareness of the university, in an attempt to boost the reputational factor of the *USNWR* rankings.

Universities also spend heavily on glossy brochures touting their institutional and faculty achievements. These are mailed to administrators at other universities, who vote on the *USNWR* surveys. Though universities (and schools within them, such as law schools) spend untold millions on these marketing publications, there is no evidence that they actually work. Most, in fact, are tossed, unopened, into the recycling bin by their recipients.[30]

In addition to expenditures that do nothing to raise the quality of teaching or research, the growing salience of rankings has led to ever new varieties of gaming through creaming and improving numbers through omission or distortion of data. A recent scholarly investigation of American law schools provides some examples. Law schools are ranked by *USNWR* based in part on the LSAT scores and GPAs of their admitted, full-time students. To improve the statistics, students with lower scores are accepted on a "part-time" or "probationary" basis, so that their scores are not included. Since the scores of transfer students are not counted, many law school admissions offices solicit students from slightly lower ranked schools to transfer in after their first year. Low student to faculty ratios also contribute to a school's score. But since those ratios are measured during the fall term, law schools encourage faculty to take leaves only during the spring term.[31]

These techniques for gaming the rankings system are by no means confined to law schools: much the same goes on at many colleges and universities.[32]

Is it all worthwhile? Some recent research shows that small differences in college rankings have much less effect on enrollment than college administrations believe, and that the resources expended to raise rankings are not commensurate with their actual impact.[33] If so, that message has yet to filter down to many university officials.

MEASURING ACADEMIC PRODUCTIVITY

In the attempt to replace judgments of quality with standardized measurement, some rankings organizations, government institutions, and university administrators have adopted as a standard the number of scholarly publications produced by a college or university's faculty, and determined the number of these publications using commercial databases that aggregate such information.[34] Here is a case where standardizing information can degrade its quality.

The first problem is that these databases are frequently unreliable: having been designed to measure output in the natural sciences, they often provide distorted information in the humanities and social sciences. In the natural sciences, and some of the behavioral sciences, new research is disseminated primarily in the form of articles published in peer-reviewed journals. But that is not the case in fields such as history, in which books remain the preeminent form of publication, and so a measurement of the number of published articles presents a distorted picture. And this is only the beginning of the problem.

When individual faculty members, or whole departments, are judged by the *number* of publications, whether in the form of articles or books, the incentive is to produce *more* publications, rather than *better* ones. Really important books may take many years to research and write. But if the incentive system rewards speed and volume of output, the result is likely to be a decline in truly significant works. That is precisely what seems to have occurred in Great Britain as a result of its Research Assessment Exercise: a great stream of publications that are both uninteresting and unread.[35] Nor is the problem confined to the humanities. In the sciences as well, evaluation solely by measured performance leads to a bias toward short-term publication rather than long-term research capacity.[36]

In academia as elsewhere, that which gets measured gets gamed. Take the practice of "impact factor measurement." Once it was recognized that not all published articles were of equal significance, techniques were developed to try to measure each article's impact. This took two forms: counting the number of times the article was cited, either on Google Scholar or on commercial databases; and considering the "impact factor" of the journal in which it was published, a factor determined in turn by the frequency with which articles in the journal were cited in the databases. (Of course, this method cannot distinguish between the following citations: "Jerry Z. Muller's illuminating and wide-ranging book on the tyranny of metrics effectively slaughters the sacred cows of so many organizations" and "Jerry Z. Muller's poorly conceived screed deserves to be ignored by all managers and social scientists." From the point of view of tabulated impact, the two statements are equivalent.) The journals were grouped by disciplines, and for most purposes, only citations in the journals within the author's discipline were counted. That too was problematic, since it tended to shortchange works of transdisciplinary interest. (Such as this one.)

Moreover, in another instance of Campbell's Law (explained in chapter 1), in an attempt to raise their citation scores, some scholars formed informal citation circles, the members of which made a point of citing one another's work as much as possible. Some lower-ranked journals actually requested that authors of accepted articles include additional citations to articles in the journal, in an attempt to improve its "impact factor."[37]

What, you might ask, is the alternative to tallying up the number of publications, the times they were cited, and the reach of the journals in which articles are published? The answer is professional judgment. In an academic department, evaluation of faculty productivity can be done by the chair or by a small committee, who, consulting with other faculty members when necessary, draw upon their knowledge, based on accumulated experience, of what constitutes significance in a book or article. In the case of major decisions, such as tenure and promotion in rank, scholars in the candidate's area of expertise are called upon to provide confidential evaluations, a more elaborate form of peer review. The numbers gathered from citation databases may be of some use in that process, but numbers too require judgment grounded in experience to evaluate their worth. That judgment grounded in professional experience is precisely what is eliminated by too great a reliance on standardized performance indicators.[38] As one expert in the use and misuse of scientific rankings puts it, "[A]ll too often, ranking systems are used as a cheap and ineffective method of assessing the productivity of individual scientists. Not only does this practice lead to inaccurate assessment, it lures scientists into pursuing high rankings first and good science second. There is a better way to evaluate the importance of a paper or the research output of an individual scholar: read it."[39]

THE VALUE AND LIMITS OF RANKINGS

Public rankings of the sort offered by *USNWR* do have some real advantages. For the uninformed, they provide at least some preliminary indication of the relative standing of various institutions. And they have prompted colleges and universities to release information of possible utility to potential students, such as the college's retention and graduation rates. What they generally fail to do is provide information that might explain *why* rates of retention and graduation are particularly high or low. A college that admits students who are well prepared will tend to have high rates of retention and graduation. But for institutions that aim to educate students who are less well prepared to begin with, "transparent" metrics make them seem to be failures, whereas they may be relatively successful given the students they have admitted. Their students are more likely to need remedial courses, are less likely to acquire a degree, and also likely to do less well in the job market. As in the case of hospitals in impoverished areas that are penalized for their relatively high rate of readmissions (which we will examine in chapter nine), colleges that serve low-income students are likely to be penalized for dealing with the particular populations who it is their mission to serve. Rankings create incentives for universities to become more like what the rankings measure. What gets measured is what gets attention. That leads to homogenization as they abandon their distinctive missions and become more like their competitors.[40]

GRADING COLLEGES: THE SCORECARD

Among the strongholds of metrics in the United States has been the Department of Education, under a succession of presidents, Republican and Democratic. During President

Obama's second term, his Department of Education set out to develop an elaborate "Postsecondary Institution Ratings System." It was intended to grade all colleges and universities, to disaggregate its data by "gender, race-ethnicity and other variables," and eventually to tie federal funds to the ratings, which were to focus on access, affordability, and outcomes, including expected earnings upon graduation. "The public should know how students fare at institutions receiving federal student aid, and this performance should be considered when we assess our investments and priorities," said Department of Education Under-Secretary Ted Mitchell. "We also need to create incentives for schools to accelerate progress toward the most important goals, like graduating low-income students and holding down costs."[41] The administration's plans for a comprehensive rating system ran into opposition from colleges and from Congress. In the end, the Department of Education settled on a stripped-down version, the "College Scorecard," which was made public in September 2015.

It was the product of good intentions, intended to address real problems in the provision of higher education. One such hazard was the extremely spotty record of for-profit institutions offering career-oriented education in fields like culinary arts, automotive repair, or health aids, which had been expanding by leaps and bounds. Some of these companies (such as Corinthian and ITT, both of which were ultimately closed down by the government) were predatory by any standard, preying upon the least informed potential students and promising that the degrees they could obtain would lead to lucrative jobs. In fact, the quality of education was often deficient, and graduates had little success in the job market. Moreover, some 90 percent of tuition flowed from the Department of Education into the coffers of the for-profit corporations, loans that were to be paid off by the student borrowers. But in reaction to a genuine problem at the low end of the for-profit sector, the department responded with far-reaching demands with consequences for *all* colleges and universities.

What the advocates of greater government accountability metrics overlook is that the very real problem of the increasing costs of college and university education is due in part to the expanding cadres of administrators, many of whom are required in order to comply with government mandates. One predictable effect of the new plan would have been to raise the costs of administration, both by diverting ever more faculty time from teaching and research into filling out forms to accumulate data, and by increasing the number of administrators to gather the forms, analyze the data, and hence supply the raw material for the government's metrics.

Some of the suggested objectives of the original plan (the Postsecondary Institution Ratings System) were mutually exclusive, while others were simply absurd. The goal of increasing college graduation rates, for example, was at odds with increasing access, since less advantaged students tend to be not only financially poorer but also worse prepared. The better prepared the students, the more likely they are to graduate on time. Thus community colleges and other institutions that provide greater access to the less prepared would have been penalized for their low graduation rates. They could, of course, have attempted to game the numbers in two ways. They could raise the standards for incoming students, increasing their likelihood of graduating—but at the price of access. Or they could respond by lowering the standards for graduation—at the price of educational quality and the market value of a degree. It might be possible to admit more economically, cognitively, and academically ill-prepared students and to ensure that more of them graduate; but only at great expense, which was at odds with another goal of the Department of Education, namely holding down educational costs.

Another metric that the colleges and universities were to supply was the average earnings of their students after graduation. That makes sense for occupationally focused, for-profit institutions, which, as we've seen, are particularly prone to overpromising and graduating students with degrees of dubious quality. But for most colleges and universities, not only is this information expensive to gather and highly unreliable—it is downright distortive. For many of the best students will go on to one or another form of professional education, insuring that their earnings will be low for at least the time they remain in school. Thus a graduate who proceeds immediately to become a greeter at Walmart would show a higher score than her fellow student who goes on to medical school. But there would be numbers to show, and hence "accountability."

Then there is the broader problem of the growing costs of college education, costs that have continued to rise well beyond the level of inflation. The issue of affordability was exacerbated by the tendency of many states to cut back their financial support for state colleges. Perhaps the least transparent element of college affordability is the actual cost of attending a particular institution, because of the gap between the sticker price and the net price. The sticker price is the official cost of tuition, room, and board; the net price is the actual amount paid by students and their parents, after accounting for financial aid based on economic need or on academic merit. The difference is often substantial, and for many people counterintuitive: because the most prestigious institutions tend to be the most well-endowed, they can afford to subsidize much of the undergraduate education of the students they admit. Thus a student poor in economic resources but rich in promise may find the actual costs of attending an elite college less than those at a less prestigious, and nominally cheaper, college. To the extent that rankings convey such information, as the College Scorecard tries to do, they provide a real service.

In keeping with Obama's announced goal of helping students and their parents to "get the most bang for your educational buck," the Scorecard highlighted three metrics: the rate of graduation, average annual cost, and "salary after attending" measured at ten years after entering college, rather than immediately after graduation.[42] The figures were problematic, in that they included only data from students who had received federal aid, which meant that the results applied only to those from lower economic backgrounds. Since those of wealthier parentage are more likely to attain greater earnings,[43] the salary figures are skewed, albeit in different directions for various colleges, depending on the mix of backgrounds of the student body. More worrisome yet is the fact that the Scorecard "makes no effort to isolate the school's contribution to earnings from what one could reasonably expect based on family incomes and test scores of its students or the level of degrees it offers."[44] Yet college outputs tend to be highly correlated with inputs: students who enter with higher levels of academic ability (and who are more often the offspring of parents with high levels of educational achievement or income) tend to be more successful on standardized assessments of college outcomes.[45] The Brookings Institution has tried to overcome this hurdle by using additional information to try to calculate the "value added," by which it means the increase in income provided by each college, in light of the available data on the backgrounds of the students entering each institution. The hope is that such metrics "will benefit the many people interested in knowing how well specific colleges are preparing students for remunerative careers."

THE MESSAGE OF THE METRICS: COLLEGE IS TO MAKE MONEY

Let us leave aside the accuracy and reliability of these metrics to explore a more important issue: the message conveyed by the metrics themselves. The College Scoreboard treats college education in purely economic terms: its sole concern is return on investment, understood as the relationship between the monetary costs of college and the increase in earnings that a degree will ultimately provide. Those are, of course, legitimate considerations: college costs eat up an increasing percentage of familial income or entail the student taking on debt; and making a living is among the most important tasks in life.

But it is not the *only* task in life, and it is an impoverished conception of college education that regards it purely in terms of its ability to enhance earnings.[46] Yet that is the ideal of education that the College Scorecard embodies and encourages, as do similar metrics. If we distinguish *training*, which is oriented to production and survival, from *education*, which is oriented to making survival meaningful, then the College Scorecard is only about the former.[47] And indeed, the Scorecard and Brookings systems tend to rank most highly institutions that are focused on engineering and technology—the stuff of production. The sort of life-long satisfaction that comes from an art history course that allows you thereafter to understand a work of art in its historical context; or a music course that trains you to listen for the theme and variations of a symphony or the jazz interpretation of a standard tune; or a literature course that heightens your appreciation of poetry; or an economics course that leaves you with an understanding of key economic institutions; or a biology course that opens your eyes to the wonders of the structures of the human body—none of these is captured by the metrics of return-on-investment. Nor is the fact that college is often a place where life-long friendships are made, often including that most important of friendships, marriage. All of these should be factored in when considering "return on investment": but because they are not measureable in quantifiable terms, they are not included.

The hazard of metrics so purely focused on monetary return on investment is that like so many metrics, they influence behavior. Already, universities at the very top of the rankings send a huge portion of their graduates into investment banking, consulting, and high-end law firms—all highly lucrative pursuits.[48] These are honorable professions, but is it really in the best interests of the nation to encourage the best and the brightest to choose these careers? One predictable effect of the weight attributed to future income in college rankings will be to incentivize institutions to channel their students into the most high-paying fields. Those whose graduates go on to careers in less remunerative fields, such as teaching or public service, will be penalized.[49]

A capitalist society depends for its flourishing on a variety of institutions that provide a counterweight to the market, with its focus on monetary gain. To prepare pupils and university students for their roles as citizens, as friends, as spouses, and above all to equip them for a life of intellectual richness—those are among the proper roles of college. Conveying marketable skills is a proper role as well. But to subordinate higher education entirely to the capacity for future earnings is to measure with a very crooked yardstick.

SCHOOLS

The quest for measureable results has been even more central to government policy regarding K-12 education. In the words of the historian of education (and erstwhile Department of Education official) Diane Ravitch, "Governors, corporate executives, the first Bush administration, and the Clinton administration agreed: They wanted measureable results; they wanted to know that the tax dollars invested in public education were getting a good return."[1] In the public sector, the show horse of metrics became "No Child Left Behind" (NCLB), a major piece of legislation enacted under George W. Bush in 2001, with bipartisan support, whose formal title was "An act to close the achievement gap with accountability, flexibility, and choice, so that no child is left behind."

THE PROBLEM AND ITS PURPORTED SOLUTION

NCLB was meant to address a real problem: despite substantial state-level efforts to equalize spending among school districts, there were persisting differences in school performance among ethnic groups. Advocates of the reforms maintained that the act would counter the lack of accountability of teachers and principals, and create incentives for improved outcomes by aligning the behavior of teachers, students, and schools with "the performance goals of the system."[2] The culprit was presumed to be a lack of professionalism among public school teachers.

The legislation grew out of more than a decade of heavy lobbying by an extraordinarily heterogeneous coalition: business groups concerned about the quality of the workforce; civil rights groups distressed by differential group achievement; and educational reformers disturbed by what they saw as the failure of public schools to educate, who demanded national standards, tests, and assessment.[3] The benefit of such measures was oversold in terms little short of utopian. William Kolberg of the National Alliance of Business asserted that "the establishment of a system of national standards, coupled with assessment, would ensure that every student leaves compulsory school with a demonstrated ability to read, write, compute and perform at world-class levels in general school subjects."[4]

The first fruit of this effort, on the federal level, was the Improving America's Schools Act, adopted under President Clinton in 1994. Meanwhile, in Texas, Governor George W. Bush became a champion of mandated testing and educational accountability. Under the NCLB act, enacted early in Bush's presidency, states were to test every student in grades 3–8 each year in math, reading, and science. The act was meant to bring all students to "academic proficiency" by 2014, and to ensure that each group of students—including blacks and Hispanics, who were singled out for comparative evaluation—within each school made "adequate yearly progress" toward proficiency each year. It imposed an escalating series of penalties and sanctions for schools in which the designated groups of students did not make adequate progress. The act was co-sponsored by Sen. Edward Kennedy, and passed both houses of Congress with both Republican and Democratic support, despite opposition from conservative Republicans antipathetic to the spread of federal power over education, and of some liberal Democrats.[5]

Yet more than a decade after its implementation, the benefits of the accountability provisions of the NCLB remain elusive. (Other aspects of NCLB—which promoted greater school choice, the creation of charter schools, and higher qualifications for teachers—seem to have been more successful, but are beyond the scope of our subject.) Its advocates grasp at any evidence of improvement on any test at any grade in any demographic group for proof of NCLB's efficacy. But test scores for primary school students went up only slightly, and no more quickly than before the legislation was enacted, and its impact upon the test scores of high school students has been more limited still.

The main impact of NCLB was to call greater attention to the "achievement gap"—the differences in academic performance among Asian, white, black, and Hispanic students.[6] Asians tended to outscore whites, who in turn tended to outscore blacks and Hispanics. Most salient was the ongoing deficiency of African American students. Eight years after the introduction of NCLB, their relative scores had not changed. Average scores on national examinations such as the National Assessment of Educational Progress tests for English and mathematics for seventeen-year-olds remained virtually unchanged from the early 1970s through 2008. In fact, the scores for each group (Asian, white, black, and Hispanic) rose somewhat, but because of the changing ethnic composition of the pupils (especially the rising percentage of Hispanic students, who tended to score less well than their Asian or white counterparts), the average national scores remained steady.[7]

UNINTENDED CONSEQUENCES

The unintended consequences of NCLB's testing-and-accountability regime are more tangible, and exemplify many of the characteristic pitfalls of metric fixation. Under NCLB, scores on standardized tests are the numerical metric by which success and failure are judged. And the stakes are high for teachers and principals, whose raises in salary and whose very jobs sometimes depend on this performance indicator. It is no wonder, then, that teachers (encouraged by their principals) divert class time toward the subjects tested—mathematic and English—and away from other subjects, such as history, social studies, art, music, and physical education. Instruction in math and English is narrowly focused on the sorts of skills required by the test, rather than broader cognitive processes: that is, students too often learn test-taking strategies rather than substantive knowledge. As depicted in the HBO series *The Wire*, a great deal of class time is devoted to practicing for tests—hardly a source of stimulation for pupils. Because students in English are taught to answer multiple choice and short-answer questions based on brief passages, the students are worse at reading extended texts and writing extended essays—much as Mathew Arnold had predicted a century and a half earlier.[8]

The problem does not lie in the use of standardized tests, which, when suitably refined, can serve as useful measures of student ability and progress. Value-added testing, which measures the changes in student performance from year to year, has real utility. It has helped to pinpoint poorly performing teachers, who have then left the system.[9] More importantly, value-added testing can be genuinely useful as a diagnostic tool, used by the teachers themselves to discover which aspects of the curriculum work and which do not. But value-added tests work best when they are "low stakes."[10] It is the emphasis placed on these tests as the major criterion for evaluating schools that creates perverse incentives, including focusing on the tests themselves at the expense of the broader goals of the institution.

High-stakes testing leads to other dysfunctions as well, such as creaming: studies of schools in Texas and in Florida showed that average achievement levels were increased by reclassifying weaker students as disabled, thus removing them from the assessment pool.[11] Or out and out cheating, as teachers alter student answers, or toss out tests by students likely to be low scorers—phenomena well documented in Atlanta, Chicago, Cleveland, Dallas, Houston, Washington, D.C., and other cities.[12] Or mayors and governors moving the goalposts by diminishing the difficulty of tests or lowering the grades required to pass them, in order to raise the pass rate and thus demonstrate the success of their educational reforms.[13]

An emphasis on measured performance through standardized tests creates another perverse outcome, as Campbell's Law (explained in chapter 1) predicts: it destroys the predictive validity of the tests themselves. Tests of performance are designed to evaluate the knowledge and ability that students have acquired in their general education. When that education becomes focused instead on developing the students' performance on the tests, the test no longer measures what it was created to evaluate. If, for example, class time is diverted to practicing multiple choice questions that resemble those on the test (perhaps by using questions from past tests), students may attain higher test scores—but without having actually learned much about the subject tested.[14]

Just a few years before the adoption of NCLB, the British government adopted its own system of metric evaluations for the school system. In 2008 a parliamentary commission looking into the system found many of the same dysfunctions as in the United States.[15]

DOUBLING DOWN ON DATA

Despite the pitfalls of the testing and accountability regime of NCLB, the Obama administration's Department of Education doubled down on accountability and metrics in K-12 education. In 2009 it introduced "Race to the Top," a program that used funds from the American Recovery and Reinvestment Act to induce states "to adopt college- and career-ready standards and assessments; build data systems that measure student growth and success; and link student achievement to teachers and administrators."[16] Whereas NCLB had focused on measuring the performance of whole schools, "Race to the Top" extended performance metrics to individual teachers. It provided funds to states and to school districts willing to adopt its metric agenda. Teachers were now to be rewarded based upon the measurable changes in the achievement of their pupils. That was known as "value-added scoring" or "student progress." It was understood that teachers could not be held responsible for how high or low the scores of their students were, since that clearly depended upon many external factors over which teachers had no control. But they were to be held responsible for how much their students learned during the year. The idea was to test pupils at the beginning and end of the academic year, to discover the "value added" (though this was adjusted for risk factors such as race and family background), and to reward teachers accordingly. In some states, value added scores came to account for half of a teacher's evaluation score. Generating the data needed to evaluate teachers under "Race to the Top" required another huge expansion of testing and assessments.[17]

The adoption of value-added performance metrics for teachers was spurred by the findings of economists. The early metrics showed that some teachers were indeed better than others, and that pupils assigned to them had greater educational success. Extrapolating from these limited metrics, some economists concluded that achievement gaps could be closed if only poor children could be taught by the top 15 percent of teachers, or if the lowest-scoring 25 percent of first-year teachers were dismissed. As time went on, however, it became clear that the yearly value-added gains tended to fade over time.[18]

PAYING FOR PERFORMANCE

Motivated by the same logic that led to "Race to the Top," school districts began to experiment with their own pay-for-performance schemes, offering bonuses to teachers based on their value-added metrics. The results were disappointing. A large-scale experiment of paying teachers for performance in New York City ran from 2007 to 2009. A study of the experiment by the economist Roland Fryer led him to conclude that there was "no evidence that teacher incentives increase student performance, attendance, or graduation, nor . . . any evidence that the incentives change student or teacher behavior."[19] So too with a 2011 study from the National Center on Performance Incentives at Vanderbilt University. It found that offering teachers in Nashville bonuses based on their value-added ratings had no discernable impact.[20] Earlier studies, dating back to the mid-1980s, had already reached the same conclusion. Despite such evidence, faith in pay-for-performance is so strong that its inadequacies must nevertheless be constantly rediscovered.[21]

The failure of pay for measured performance schemes to achieve results has not stopped the federal government from pouring ever greater resources into such efforts. In 2010, for example, the Department of Education selected sixty-two programs in twenty-seven states to receive some 1.2 billion dollars over the course of five years from its Teacher Incentive Fund. Nor is the United States unique in such efforts. Similar schemes to link teacher raises, tenure, and promotion to measured performance were undertaken in the United Kingdom, Portugal, Australia, Chile, Mexico, Israel, and India.[22]

THE NEVER-CLOSING "ACHIEVEMENT GAP"

Perhaps the preeminent concern of advocates of one or another form of metrics in the field of American education is the disparity in educational attainment among ethnically or racially defined groupings. That was a major motive behind the predecessors of "No Child Left Behind" and of the act itself, and it remained central to the policy of the Department of Education during the Obama administration, and to the reauthorized revision of NCLB, the "Every Student Succeeds Act," passed in late 2015. (Like "No Child Left Behind" or "Operation Iraqi Freedom," the title of the act expressed a pious hope.) Nor is that concern confined to the federal level: it is salient in the educational policy of many states and countless municipalities, and it dominates the agenda of teachers colleges. Schools are increasingly conceived as "gap-closing factories."[23]

Yet it is striking that after decades of gathering and publicizing these metrics, the outcome has remained more or less unchanged. The positions of blacks and Hispanics relative to whites are remarkably stable. While there have been some minor fluctuations when students are measured in grades 4 and 8, there is almost no change in the ultimate result—the metrics in grade 12, that is, at the end of high school.

Pupils throughout the United States are administered tests of reading and mathematics in grades 4, 8, and 12. These are the NAEP (National Assessment of Educational Progress) tests. Experts regard them as relatively reliable indicators of performance, because, unlike some other tests, they involve "low stakes": that is to say, the fortunes of the students, the teachers, or the schools are not affected by the outcomes, and so there is less incentive for teachers to skim the testing pool, to teach to the test, or to fabricate results. The National Center for Educational Statistics publishes an annual report, *Status and Trends in the Educational Achievement of Racial and Ethnic Groups*, comparing the relative rates of achievement among Asians, whites, Hispanics, and blacks (as well as some subdivisions of each of these groups) over time.

Its findings are telling. For those who took the test in grade 12, the reading achievement gap between whites and Hispanics (22 points on a scale of 500, where the average score in 2013 was 288) was no different in 2013 than it had been in 1992. The gap between whites and blacks was actually *larger* in 2013 (30 points) than it had been in 1992 (24 points). As for math, the report compares the relative performance of each group in 2005, 2009, and 2013. The result: the gap in scores between whites and their black and Hispanic peers remained unchanged.[24]

The inability of the schools to influence the relative level of educational attainment should come as no surprise. Since at least the Coleman Report, "Equal Educational Opportunity" (1966) commissioned during the Johnson administration, it has been known that the output of schools depends largely upon the inputs: student performance correlates closely to the social, economic, and educational attainment of their parents.[25] "Good schools" tend to be those populated by pupils who are brighter, more curious, and more self-controlled; and these tend to be the offspring of people who are themselves relatively bright, curious, and self-disciplined. Since these traits are conducive to success, and since they tend to be passed down in families, more successful parents tend to send to schools children who are more likely to achieve educationally.

General improvements in schooling do not therefore lead to greater equality of outcomes. As the political scientist Edward Banfield noted a generation ago, "*All* education favors the middle- and upper-class child, because to be middle- or upper-class is to have qualities that make one particularly educable." Improvements in the quality of schools may elevate overall educational outcomes, but they tend to increase, rather than diminish, the gap in achievement between children from families with different levels of human capital.[26]

Such outcomes might lead one to conclude that the achievement gap cannot in fact be closed by education—and that the reasons lie beyond the schoolhouse door. Yet measuring continues unabated. That is perhaps because, as Banfield noted, the idea that some problems are insoluble is morally unacceptable to a substantial portion of educated Americans.[27] When it comes to gaps in school achievement, it seems that in the absence of discernable progress in *results*, the resources devoted to ongoing *measurement* becomes itself a sign of moral earnestness.

THE COSTS OF ATTEMPTED GAP-CLOSING

Of course, the scores on English and math achievement tests cannot measure the full benefits of K-12 education. That is not because the NAEP scores are distorted or insignificant. They *do* provide a useful measure of student knowledge of the subjects tested. But there is much more to school than the learning of English and mathematics: not only other academic subjects but also the stimulation of interest in the world, and the cultivation of habits of behavior (self-control, perseverance, ability to cooperate with others) that increase the likelihood of success in the adult world. Development of these noncognitive qualities may well be going on in classrooms and schools without being reflected in performance metrics based on test scores.[28]

In fact, the growing emphasis on testing students in English and math as early as kindergarten may come at the expense of nonacademic activities, such as creative play and the arts, that contribute to individual development but are not easily measured.[29] Moreover, though exposing students to better teachers may lead to gains in academic achievement, those gains tend to fade away over time. The noncognitive gains, however, appear to persist.[30] Character development matters—which has led some legislatures to try to incorporate measurement of character into their accountability systems![31]

The costs of trying to use metrics to turn schools into gap-closing factories are therefore not only monetary. The broader mission of schools to instruct in history and in civics is neglected as attention is focused on attempting to improve the reading and math scores of lower-performing groups. Pedagogic strategies that may be effective for lower-achieving students (such as longer school days and shorter summer vacations) are extended to students for whom these strategies are counterproductive. And resources are diverted away from maximizing learning on the part of the more gifted and talented—who may in fact hold the key to national economic performance.[32]

The emphasis on measuring the achievement gap and the pressure to close it has other troubling effects. One is the blame heaped upon teachers and schools for their failure to accomplish what may be beyond their reach, and for reasons that have little to do with their own limitations. The logic of NCLB, "Race to the Top," and similar programs, places the responsibility for closing achievement gaps on those who may have neither the power nor the ability to do so. That itself is a recipe for the demoralization of teachers. Add to that the dilemma presented to teachers: pursuing the multiple aims of education versus teaching to the test; following their broad vocational mission versus adhering to the narrow criteria upon which they are to be remunerated. Whichever course they choose, they lose. In addition, many teachers perceive the regimen created by the culture of testing and measured accountability as robbing them of their autonomy, and of the ability to use their discretion and creativity in designing and implementing the curriculum of their students. The result has been a wave of retirements by experienced teachers, and a movement by the more creative away from public and toward private schools, which are not bound by the regime of metric accountability.[33]

Thus, the self-congratulations of those who insist upon rewarding measured educational performance in order to close achievement gaps come at the expense of those actually engaged in trying to educate children. Not everything that can be measured can be improved—at least, not by measurement.

MEDICINE

Nowhere are metrics in greater vogue than in the field of medicine. Nowhere, perhaps, are they more promising. And the stakes are high.

But here too, metrics play a variety of roles—some genuinely useful, some of more dubious worth.

One role is informational and diagnostic: the process of keeping track of various methods and procedures, and then comparing the outcomes, makes it possible to determine which are most successful. The successful methods and procedures can then be followed by others.

Another is publicly reported metrics, intended to provide transparency to consumers, and a basis for comparison and competition among providers.

Yet another is pay-for-performance, in which accountability is backed up with monetary rewards or penalties. Advocates of the use of metrics in medicine often discuss these very different roles in the same breath.

The great push in recent decades has been for metrics to be used not only to improve safety and effectiveness but also to contain costs.

THE FINANCIAL PUSH TO CONTROL COSTS

The impetus to employ metrics to control costs has come from a number of directions, and arises from a variety of motives. For years, medical costs have been rising more quickly than national income, and they are projected to continue to do so for at least the next decade: in 2014, the health sector made up 17.5 percent of the American economy, and is expected to reach 20.1 percent by 2025. There are some good reasons for that: health expenditure is what economists call a "luxury good"—the richer people are, the more they are willing to spend on it. Then there is the fact that as the baby boom generation ages, that large cohort of the population is reaching the age of maximal medical expenditures. Add to that the availability of more specialty drugs and the faster growth in drug prices. The adoption of the Affordable Care Act meant that an ever higher percentage of healthcare spending in the United States would be by the government, with the share of total health expenditures paid for by federal, state, and local governments projected to increase to 47 percent by 2025.[1]

The increasing cost of healthcare has led both private insurers and government insurers (the National Health Service in Britain; and Medicare, Medicaid, and the Veterans Administration in the United States) to put pressure on doctors and hospitals to lower reimbursement rates and to improve outcomes. At the same time as pressure to control costs is escalating, the new technology of electronic health records has made the collection of medical data more readily obtainable, creating a temptation to exploit the data to identify problems. The upshot has been a huge increase in public reporting and in pay-for-performance, both of which were hailed as cures for the ills of the healthcare system in the United States and abroad. The problems are real enough: third-party payers, whether insurance companies or government agencies such as Medicaid and Medicare, do need reliable evidence that doctors and hospitals are providing services in an effective and cost-efficient manner. But the touted cures have sometimes proved almost as bad as the diseases they were meant to treat.

RANKING THE AMERICAN MEDICAL SYSTEM

But before we examine those purported cures, it is worth visiting the most influential performance metrics used to characterize the American healthcare system, metrics frequently cited as evidence of the need for more accountability and for paying for measured performance. They come from the World Health Organization's "World Health Report 2000," which ranked the United States healthcare system as thirty-seventh among the nations of the world, and stated, "It is hard to ignore that ... the United States was number 1 in terms of healthcare spending per capita but ranked 39th for infant mortality, 43rd for adult female mortality, 42nd for adult male mortality, and 36th for life expectancy."[2] Scott W. Atlas, a physician and healthcare analyst, has scrutinized and contextualized these claims, which turn out to be more than a little misleading.

Most of us assume that the WHO rankings measured the overall level of health. But actual health outcomes accounted for only 25 percent of the ranking scale. Half of the points awarded were for egalitarianism: 25 percent for "health distribution," and another 25 percent for "financial fairness," where "fairness" was defined as having everyone pay the same percent of their income for healthcare. That is, only a system in which the richer you are, the more you pay for healthcare was deemed fair. The criterion, in short, was ideological. The fact that there was a number attached (37th) gave it the appearance of objectivity and reliability.[3] But in fact, the overall performance ranking is deceptive.

What about the figures for mortality and life expectancy? These, it turns out, are influenced in large part by factors *outside* the medical system, factors having to do with culture and styles of life. Obesity tends to foster chronic and debilitating illnesses such as type-II diabetes and heart disease—and Americans are, on average, more obese than citizens of other nations (though some of the others are catching up quickly). Cigarette smoking also contributes mightily to heart disease, cancer, and other ailments, and may do so decades after a person gives up the habit. Americans, it turns out, were heavy smokers by international standards for generations, up through the 1980s. Americans have disproportionately high rates of death from gunshot wounds, another factor that is lamentable, but has almost nothing to do with the medical system.[4] Moreover, the United States is an ethnically heterogeneous country, and some ethnic groups (such as African Americans) have disproportionately high rates of infant mortality, reflecting social, cultural, and possibly genetic factors.[5] In short, many of the problems of American health are a function not of the medical system but of social and cultural factors *beyond* the medical system. When it comes to diagnosing and treating disease, Atlas notes, American medicine is among the best in the world.[6]

Here, as in other areas such as education and public safety, many of the most important factors making for relative success or failure lie beyond the formal systems that we try to measure and hold accountable. Getting enough exercise; eating right; keeping firearms out of irresponsible hands; and refraining from smoking, overconsumption of alcohol, drugs, and hazardous sex—these are the main factors contributing to health and longevity. Physicians and public health officials should try to influence them—and try they do. But these life-style patterns are largely matters beyond their control. We must keep that in mind in evaluating the purported failures of American medicine. Yet even if we take the alarmist metrics of the WHO report with a grain of salt, it is still true that healthcare in the United States is expensive and open to improvement.

METRICS AS SOLUTION

Perhaps the most popular trend in American health policy is the promotion of performance metrics, accountability, and transparency. Measured performance is supposed to allow practitioners to better assess clinical practices and to track their implementation; allow insurers to reward success and penalize failure; and through ratings and report cards, create transparency in ways that will allow patients to make more informed choices about medical providers.

One booster is Michael E. Porter of the Harvard Business School, whose "value agenda" includes the application of management metrics to medicine. Porter claims,

> Rapid improvement in any field requires measuring re-sults—a familiar principle in management. Teams improve and excel by tracking progress over time and comparing their performance to that of peers inside and outside their organization. Indeed, rigorous measurement of value (outcomes and costs) is perhaps the single most important step in improving health care. Wherever we see systematic measurement of results in health care—no matter what the country—we see those results improve.[7]

Porter is a great believer in public reporting of outcomes, which is thought to provide a powerful incentive for improving performance. That makes sense—in theory.

THREE TALES OF SUCCESS

Porter points to the Cleveland Clinic as a pioneer of his recommended approach. The clinic annually publishes fourteen "outcome books" that document its performance in treating a remarkable variety of ailments. A look at those documents (which are available online) indicates a high rate of success in each category. And the Cleveland Clinic attracts patients from around the world.

A convincing example of the potential virtues of medical metrics, also touted by Michael Porter, comes from the Geisinger Health System, a physician-led, not-for-profit, integrated system that serves some 2.6 million people in Pennsylvania, many of them rural and poor. Geisinger is a showcase for progressive healthcare in the United States—and with good reason.[8] A pioneer in the use of electronic health records, Geisinger in 1995 began to invest more than $100 million in its electronic health records system, and gave doctors an incentive to have their patients sign up for an online portal. That system allows for the ready transmission of information to providers in the system, and for the monitoring of performance of the units, including individual physicians. The system employs nurse case-managers for patients at high risk, who educate patients about their condition, monitor them, review their care plans and medications, and make follow-up appointments. The two most costly and widespread conditions in American healthcare are diabetes and heart disease. In the Geisinger system, patients with such conditions are treated by an integrated team of physicians and physician assistants, pharmacists, dieticians, and more. Rather than parceling out treatment to a series of providers, whose contact with one another might be minimal, Geisinger employs a more holistic approach. Some 20 percent of physician compensation is tied to goals related to cutting costs, improving quality of care, and patient satisfaction, while the other 80 percent of compensation is based on fee-for-service. Through its panoply of innovative programs, Geisinger has succeeded in lowering costs and improving patient outcomes.

One of the more unequivocally successful uses of metrics in medicine is the use of performance measures to reduce hospital-induced infections acquired from "central lines." Central lines are the flexible catheter tubes inserted into a large vein through the neck or chest, as a conduit for medicines, nutrients, and fluids. Central lines are among the most common elements of modern hospital medicine—and, until recently, one that contributed the most to complications. That is because the catheters provide a ready avenue of infection, infections that are deadly in the worst cases, and are costly to treat even in the best cases. In 2001 it was estimated that in the United States there were some 82,000 blood infections associated with central lines. The costs per infection ranged from $12,000 to $56,000. Almost 32,000 people died.[9]

Since then, the rate of acquired infections has dropped dramatically, thanks in no small part to the efforts of Peter J. Pronovost, a critical-care specialist at Johns Hopkins University hospital in Baltimore. Together with his colleagues, he developed a program based on a checklist of five standard yet simple procedures that in combination reduced the likelihood of central-line-induced infection. After applying his program at Johns Hopkins, Pronovost supervised its application at a hospital system in Michigan, in what was known as the "Michigan Keystone ICU Project." Similar programs have since been implemented throughout the United States, as well as in England and Spain. The results have been dramatic: blood stream infections dropped by 66 percent, saving thousands of lives and millions of dollars.

The Keystone project includes gathering monthly data on infection rates, which are reported to the leaders of intensive care units and to top hospital officials. The results are discussed with the larger staff, with an eye to learning from mistakes. This is an instance of *diagnostic* metrics. It provides data that can be used by a practitioner (physician), or internally within an institution (hospital), or shared among practitioners and institutions to discover what is working and what is not, and to use that information to improve performance.

The Keystone project involved extensive use of diagnostic metrics, as well as some psychic incentives in the form of peer pressure. Pronovost himself accounts for its success by the fact that the project worked through clinical communities, working toward common professional goals and treating central line–induced infections as a solvable social problem. Seeing their infection rate compared to other hospitals also created peer pressure, to try to keep up with or exceed the success rate of peer institutions.

WHAT SHOULD WE CONCLUDE FROM THESE SUCCESSES?

The Cleveland Clinic, Geisinger, and the Keystone project are frequently cited as proof of the efficacy of measuring performance, and with reason. Yet when we dig more deeply, we find that the metrics matter because of the way they are embedded into a larger institutional culture.

Is the success of the Cleveland Clinic a function of the fact that the Clinic publishes its outcomes? Or is the Clinic eager to publicize its outcomes precisely because they are so impressive? In fact, the Cleveland Clinic was one of the world's great medical institutions before the rise of performance metrics, and it maintains that standing in the age of performance metrics. But to conclude that there is a causal relationship between the clinic's quality and the publication of its performance metrics is to fall prey to the fallacy of *post hoc ergo propter hoc*. The success may have far more to do with local conditions—the ways in which the organizational culture of the Cleveland Clinic makes use of metrics—than with quality measurement per se.[10]

Metrics at Geisinger are effective because of the way in which they are embedded in a larger system. Crucially, the establishment of measurement criteria and the evaluation of performance are done by teams that include physicians as well as administrators. The metrics of performance, therefore, are neither imposed nor evaluated from above by administrators devoid of firsthand knowledge. They are based on collaboration and peer review. Geisinger also uses its metrics to continuously improve its performance in outpatient care for a variety of conditions. Here is how Glenn D. Steele, a physician who presided over the transformation of the Geisinger system as CEO, accounts for its successes: "Our new care pathways were effective because they were led by physicians, enabled by real-time data-based feedback, and primarily focused on improving the quality of patient care," which "fundamentally motivated our physicians to change their behavior." Crucial too was the fact that "the men and women who actually work in the service lines themselves chose which care processes to change. Involving them directly in decision making secured their buy-in and made success more likely." What we can learn from the Geisinger example is the importance of having providers develop and monitor performance measures. The fact that the measures were in keeping with their own professional sense of mission was crucial.

Peter Pronovost, who spearheaded the reduction of central line infections, believes that "The Keystone ICU project demonstrated the potential of voluntary efforts that rely on intrinsic motivation through peer norms and professionalism." He's not opposed to supplementing these appeals with public reporting and monetary incentives. But his own interpretation is that the improvement in medical outcomes was brought about primarily by "a shift in clinicians' belief—by showing them that the rate of infection was not inevitable and could be controlled, in a way that appealed to their professional ethos as doctors and nurses."

However, the conclusion drawn by the U.S. government's Centers for Medicare and Medicaid Services was to initiate public reporting of the infection rates in 2011, and a year later, to begin penalizing hospitals with higher infection rates by withholding reimbursements. That created a structure of incentives very different from the institutional successes we've examined so far, which relied more on intrinsic than extrinsic motivations.

THE BROADER PICTURE: METRICS, PAY-FOR-PERFORMANCE, RANKINGS, AND REPORT CARDS

When we dig deeper into the record of performance metrics in the field of medicine, the successes of the Cleveland Clinic, Geisinger, and Keystone seem more the exception than the rule.

Most of the professionals who write about medical metrics have a vested interest in the effectiveness of measuring performance. Their careers are based in no small part on the efficacy of gathering and analyzing data. Thus the many studies demonstrating the *lack* of efficacy or *very limited* efficacy of publicly released accountability metrics should be read as testimony against interest. The healthcare journals and academic literature are replete with such studies, as we'll see. To be sure, they more often end with a plea for more data, more studies, and more refined metrics, rather than a bald declaration that metrics have proved futile.[11] But the fact that these studies in failure come from those who are by no means antipathetic to measured performance makes them all the more significant.[12]

The argument for accountability and transparency is based on the premise that the public release of metrics of success and failure will influence the behavior of patients, professionals, and organizations. Patients will act as consumers, comparing the cost of care with relative success rates. Doctors will recommend patients to specialists with high performance scores. Insurers will flock to hospitals and providers who supply the best care at the lowest price. Doctors and hospitals will feel pressure to improve their scores, lest their reputation and their income suffer.[13]

To test whether the theory holds true in reality, a group of experts from the Scientific Institute for Quality of Healthcare (IQ Healthcare), at the Radboud University Nijmegen Medical Centre in the Netherlands, examined the existing evidence to see how widely accessible information on research pertaining to a variety of health issues impacted provider and patient/consumer behavior as well as patient outcomes. They included controlled before-and-after studies, which compare behavior before and after the introduction of publicly available medical metrics for a wide range of conditions, such as heart attacks. The Dutch experts found that in some cases, hospitals did indeed initiate improvements in their *processes*. But, in contradiction to the prediction of accountability advocates, there was no lasting effect on patient *outcomes*.

That may be a product of the relationship between medical research and medical practice. The populations upon which medical research is based differ from the real populations that doctors and hospitals treat. Plausible medical interventions (such as controlling blood sugar to try to prevent diabetes) are tested on relatively small groups of patients, and to isolate the effects of the intervention, such studies deliberately exclude patients with multiple medical problems. But in the real world, patients often *do* have multiple medical problems (comorbidities), so that the effect of the tested intervention often disappears. That might explain why simply following the recommended procedures does not necessarily lead to improved outcomes.[14]

Nor, according to the Dutch experts, did the publication of metrics affect patient behavior in choosing a provider or hospital. Their conclusion: "The small body of evidence available provides no consistent evidence that the public release of performance data changes consumer behavior or improves care."[15]

Another prominent use of metrics is in pay-for-performance (P4P) schemes. Here the incentive structure is straightforward: physicians receive some substantial part of their remuneration for having reached some measured target, such as following recommended procedures (checklists), or cutting costs, or improving outcomes.

In the United Kingdom, the National Health Service (NHS) began to adopt P4P as a key feature of its compensation arrangements with primary care physicians in the mid-1990s, a feature that was extended by the Tony Blair administration. In the United States, private health plans and employer groups have increasingly adopted P4P programs, as have state governments. And P4P provisions are an important part of the remuneration that physicians receive from Medicare as part of the Affordable Care Act of 2010.[16] Medicare administrators have tried to reward a variety of measured outcomes, including surgical results, using as a criterion the rate of survival until thirty days after surgery.

Another prominent form of medical metrics is the public ranking of doctors and hospitals in the form of "medical report cards." New York State pioneered the publication of such data; in England, the Department of Health began in 2001 to publish annual "star ratings" for public healthcare organizations; and England recently became the first country to mandate the publication of "outcome data" for surgeons across nine surgical specialties. In 2015 the American news reporting organization ProPublica published the complication rates for some 17,000 surgeons across the United States.[17] Report cards and rankings are also published by the nonprofit "Joint Commission" on medical accreditation, and by private profit-making rankings, such as the website *Healthgrades* or *US News and World Report*. The notion behind all of these groups is that doctors and hospitals will have an incentive to perform better in order to improve their reputations for safety and efficacy, and ultimately their market share of the potential patient population. For hospitals, these rankings are important for status and "brand management."[18]

There is now a large social scientific literature on the impact of pay-for-performance and public performance metrics in the United States, the United Kingdom, and elsewhere. What is quite astonishing is how often these techniques—so obviously effective according to economic theory—have no discernable effect on outcomes.[19]

A recent study in the *Annals of Internal Medicine*, for example, looked at the fate of Medicare patients in the years since public reporting of hospital mortality rates began in 2009. According to the authors, "We found that public reporting of mortality rates has had no impact on patient outcomes. We looked at every subgroup. We even examined those that were labeled as bad performers to see if they would improve more quickly. They didn't. In fact, if you were going to be faithful to the data, you would conclude that public reporting slowed down the rate of improvement in patient outcomes."[20] As if that were not enough of a problem, many of these public rankings, such as ProPublica's surgical report card, are based on what experts regard as dubious criteria, as likely to be misleading as genuinely illuminating.[21]

Another recent report, this time from the Rand Corporation, came to similar conclusions. Most studies of pay-for-performance, it noted, examined process and intermediate outcomes rather than final outcomes, that is, whether the patient recovered. "Overall," it reports, "studies with stronger methodological designs were less likely to identify significant improvements associated with pay-for-performance programs. And identified effects were relatively small."[22] Nor was this finding new. Social scientists who studied pay-for-performance schemes in the public sector in the 1990s concluded that they were ineffective. Yet such schemes keep getting introduced: a triumph of hope over experience, or of consultants peddling the same old nostrums.[23]

When metrics used for public rankings or pay-for-performance *do* affect outcomes, it is often in ways that are unintended and counterproductive. And whether productive or unproductive, they typically involve huge costs, costs that are rarely considered by the advocates of pay-for-performance or transparency metrics.

Among the intrinsic problems of P4P and public rankings are goal diversion. As a report from Britain notes, P4P programs "can reward only what can be measured and attributed, a limitation that can lead to less holistic care and inappropriate concentration of the doctor's gaze on what can be measured rather than what is important." The British P4P program led to lower quality of care for those medical conditions that were *not* part of the program. In short, it leads to "treating to the test." And it is simply impossible to provide reliable criteria of measurement for the treatment of many patients, such as the frail elderly, who suffer from multiple, chronic conditions.[24]

Physician report cards create as many problems as they solve. Take the phenomenon of risk-aversion. Numerous studies have shown that cardiac surgeons became less willing to operate on severely ill patients in need of surgery after the introduction of publicly available metrics. In New York State, for example, the report cards for surgeons report on postoperative mortality rates for coronary bypass surgery, that is, what percentage of the patients operated upon remain alive thirty days after the procedure. After the metrics were instituted, the mortality rates did indeed decline—which seems like a positive development. But only those patients who were operated upon were included in the metric. The patients who the surgeons *declined* to operate on because they were more high-risk—and hence would bring down the surgeon's score—were not included in the metrics. Some of these sicker patients were referred to the Cleveland Clinic, and so the outcomes of their procedures did not show up in the New York metrics. As a result of this "case selection bias" (that is, creaming) some sicker patients were simply not operated on. Nor is it clear that the improvement in postoperative outcomes in New York State was a result of the publication of the metrics. It turns out that the same improvement occurred in the neighboring state of Massachusetts, where there was no public reporting of data.[25]

The phenomenon of risk-aversion means that some patients whose lives might be saved by a risky operation are simply never operated upon. But there is also the reverse problem, that of overly aggressive care to meet metric targets. Patients whose operations are not successful may be kept alive for the requisite thirty days to improve their hospital's mortality data, a prolongation that is both costly and inhumane.[26]

To be sure, there are some real advantages to publicly available metrics of surgeon success and of hospital mortality rates. Their publication can point out very poor performers, who may then cease practicing, in the case of surgeons—a sifting process all the more valuable in a profession in which practitioners are reluctant to dismiss incompetent fellow members of the guild. Or the lower-level performers can take steps to improve their measured performance, in the case of hospitals. But the tendency here, as with so many performance metrics, is to glean the low-hanging fruit, and then expect a continuingly bountiful harvest. That is to say, there are immediate benefits to discovering poorly performing outliers.[27] The problem is that the metrics continue to get collected from everyone. And at some point the marginal costs exceed the marginal benefits.

Just how costly and burdensome the pursuit of ever more medical metrics has become is evident in a recent report from the Institute of Medicine.[28] At major medical centers, the cost of reporting quality measures to government regulators and insurers amounted to 1 percent of net revenue. Administrative costs for measurement and related activities are estimated at $190 billion per year. Then there is the unmeasureable cost of providers entering data into the government's Patient Quality Reporting Systems. Larger medical practices must pay external firms to enter the data; in smaller practices, it is sometimes left to the physicians themselves. In addition to the tangible costs of gathering, inputting, and processing this tsunami of data, there are the incalculable opportunity costs of what doctors and other clinicians might have done with the time they must devote to inputting data. Moreover, the time invested is largely uncalculated and uncompensated. It typically falls out of consideration when medical costs are discussed.[29] "Ironically," the Institute of Medicine study reports, "the rapid proliferation of interest, support, and capacity for new measurement efforts for a variety of purposes—including performance assessment and improvement, public and funder reporting, and internal improvement initiatives—has blunted the effectiveness of those efforts."

Donald M. Berwick is a leading advocate of improvement through measurement who served as the Administrator of the Centers for Medicare and Medicaid from 2010 to 2011. Reporting requirements have become so burdensome and redundant that Dr. Berwick recently declared, "We need to stop excessive measurement. . . . I vote for a 50 percent reduction in all metrics currently being used."[30]

Add to this the psychic costs of treating medicine as if it were primarily a profit-making enterprise. Berwick captured this brilliantly in his article, "The Toxicity of Pay for Performance":

> *"Pay for performance"* reduces *intrinsic motivation.* Many tasks, especially in health care, are potentially intrinsically satisfying. Relieving pain, answering questions, exercising manual dexterity, being confided in, working on a profes-

sional team, solving puzzles, and experiencing the role of a trusted authority—these are not at all bad ways to spend part of one's day at work. Pride and joy in the work of caring is among the many motivations that do result in "performance" among health care professionals. In the rancorous debates about compensation, fees, and reimbursement that so occupy the time of health care leaders and clinicians today, it is all too easy to neglect, or even to doubt, the fact that nonfinancial and intrinsic rewards are important in the work of medical care. Unfortunately, neglecting intrinsic satisfiers in work can inadvertently diminish them.[31]

Berwick's article appeared more than two decades ago. It seems to have had no effect. The tidal wave of pay-for-performance continues to rise.

A TEST CASE: REDUCING READMISSIONS

Among the most touted uses of measurement are Medicare's metrics for unplanned readmissions to hospitals within thirty days of discharge, which demonstrates both the promise and the problems of metrics. Hospital admissions are expensive, and one motive has been to reduce costs. Readmissions were also thought to be a result of inadequate patient care, and so lowering the number of admissions would be a sign of improved care. In 2009, Medicare began public reporting by all acute care hospitals of readmission rates within thirty days of discharge, a form of transparency metrics. The thirty-day readmission metric covered patients who had been treated for major medical conditions (heart attacks, heart failure, strokes, pneumonia, chronic obstructive pulmonary disease, coronary artery bypass), and two common surgical procedures, hip or knee replacements. (The metrics are publicized on Medicare's "Hospital Compare" website.) Then in 2012, Medicare went from public reporting to paying for performance, by imposing financial penalties on hospitals with higher than average rates.[32] The public reporting of performance and the monetary penalization of failure served as a stimulus for hospitals to take measures to limit readmissions and, since hospital admissions are expensive, to cut costs. Hospitals began taking additional steps to try to ensure that patients leaving the hospital would not have to return. That included better coordination with primary care providers, and trying to ensure that patients had access to the medicines prescribed to them. The fines levied upon low-performing hospitals were intended to motivate them to provide better care for their patients, so that they would not have to return to the hospital.

Hospital readmissions have indeed declined, a much-touted success for performance metrics. But how much of that success is real?

The falling rate of reported readmissions was due in part to gaming the system: instead of formally admitting returning patients, hospitals placed them on "observation status," under which the patient stays in the hospital for a period of time (up to several days), and is billed for outpatient services rather than an inpatient "admission." Alternatively, the returning patients were treated in the emergency room. Between 2006 and 2013, such observation stays for Medicare patients increased by 96 percent. That meant that about half the drop in readmissions was actually due to patients who had in fact returned to the hospital but were treated as outpatients. (To complicate matters, a later analysis indicated that the hospitals that lowered their readmission rates were not the ones that increased the number of patients under observation.) The metrics of readmission thus improved, but not necessarily the quality of patient care.

Not all hospitals gamed the system: some really did examine and refine their procedures to actually improve patient outcomes and lower Medicare costs by reducing readmissions. But others simply improved their ability to manipulate the labels under which patients were categorized in judging performance.[33]

There were other negative consequences. As of 2015, about three-quarters of the reporting hospitals were penalized by Medicare. Tellingly, major teaching hospitals—which tend to see more difficult patients—were disproportionately affected.[34] So were hospitals in poverty-stricken areas, where patients were less likely to be well taken care of (or to take care of themselves) after their initial discharge from the hospital.[35] Attaining the goal of reduced admissions depends not only on the steps that the hospital takes to educate the patient and provide necessary medications, but also on many factors over which the hospital has little control: the patient's underlying physical and mental health, social support system, and behavior. Such factors point to another recurrent issue with medical metrics: hospitals serve very different patient populations, some of whom are more prone to illness and less able to take care of themselves once discharged. Pay-for-performance schemes try to compensate for this by what is known as "risk adjustment." But calculations of the degree of risk are at least as prone to mismeasurement and manipulation as other metrics. In the end, hospitals that serve the most challenging patient population are most likely to be penalized.[36] As in the case of schools punished for the poor performance of their students on standardized tests, by penalizing the least successful hospitals, performance metrics may end up exacerbating inequalities in the distribution of resources—hardly a contribution to the public health they are supposed to improve.

A BALANCE SHEET

Most healthcare delivery organizations now use metrics for quality improvement purposes, from bettering outcomes for specific procedures to optimizing operations for an entire institution. This internal use of metrics of performance is of great value in helping hospitals and other medical institutions to enhance the safety and efficacy of their medical care. But metrics tend to be most successful for those interventions and outcomes that are almost entirely controlled by and within the organization's medical system, as in the case of checklists of procedures to minimize central line–induced infections. When the outcomes are dependent upon more wide-ranging factors (such as patient behavior outside the doctor's office and the hospital), they become more difficult to attribute to the efforts or failures of the medical system. Geisinger's success in managing population health offers hope. But it does so in a context in which diagnostic metrics play a part in a larger institutional culture, in which such metrics are developed and evaluated by practitioners, in keeping with their professional ethos.

The use of metrics to reward performance, either through monetary or reputational rewards, is much more problematic. There is increasing resort to metrics tied to monetary incentives and public rankings. Whether they are adding or subtracting to the costs and benefits of healthcare remains an open question.

POLICING

Like medicine, policing has been transformed in recent decades by the use of metrics. Here too the stakes are high: the fate of cities rests in no small part on the public's perception of its safety, and mayors often stake their reelection on their ability to control crime or to bring down the crime rate. When the public and its politicians think of public safety, they think of the police, who are held responsible for the level of crime. However, like health and its relationship to the medical system, or education and its relationship to the school system, public safety is only partially dependent on the effectiveness of the police. It depends in part on other elements of the justice system: on the public prosecutors, the judiciary, and the penal and parole systems. It depends in good part on the propensity of the local population to engage in criminal activity, and that in turn depends on broader economic, ethnic, and cultural factors.[1] And public safety also depends on the ease of committing crime. Some of the decline in crime in recent decades is a product of private actions by property owners. The opportunity for car theft, burglary, and other crimes has been radically reduced by defensive measures undertaken by millions of private individuals, whose acquisition of improved car alarms and home alarms has made these crimes more difficult. In addition, there are about one million people employed by private security firms in the United States.

Violent crime has fallen in the United States since the early 1990s. Rightly or wrongly, much of that decline is commonly attributed to changes in policing. And the major change in policing has involved the increased use of metrics, above all in the form of Compstat. Here is a case where diagnostic metrics for internal use have proved genuinely useful. But then again, the use of publicly released metrics to bolster the reputations of politicians and police chiefs has also created incentives for gaming and fudging the numbers, and for counterproductive diversion of effort.

Compstat (which originally stood for "computer statistics") is a crime analysis and accountability system, first developed by the New York Police Department in 1994. Pioneered under Police Commissioner William J. Bratton, Compstat uses Geographical Information Systems (GIS) to track the incidence of crime. It involves the collection, analysis, and mapping of crime data in a rapid time-frame to discover crime patterns, as well as entailing weekly meetings at which police managers are held accountable for the results in their precinct. The data are used to pinpoint hot spots in which crime is concentrated, and to deploy police resources accordingly. In the decades since it was rolled out in New York, some variation of Compstat has been adopted in many large American cities.[2] Compstat does seem to have contributed to the decline in reported crime—and indeed, to the decline of crime itself.

Yet in city after city, there have been questions about the accuracy and reliability of crime statistics. Insofar as Compstat is a system of informational and indicative metrics, it seems genuinely useful. But when the mayor pressures the top brass to show improvements in the overall numbers, and that pressure, in turn, is placed on the district commanders who are led to believe that their career advancement depends on a steady diminution in crime, the message sometimes heard by lower-level police officers is that they will be penalized for an increase in reported crime. And that creates pressures for fudging the numbers.

Such problems preceded the rise of Compstat and exist independent of it. In 1976 the social psychologist Donald T. Campbell (of Campbell's Law, see chapter 1) noted that President Richard Nixon's declared crackdown on crime "had as its main effect the corruption of crime-rate indicators, achieved through underrecording and downgrading the crimes to less serious classifications."[3] And that continues. The most widely reported metric of crime is the Federal Bureau of Investigation's Uniform Crime Report. Based upon the reports from each city, the FBI compiles data on four major violent crimes (homicide, rape, aggravated assault, and robbery) and four major property crimes (burglary, theft, motor vehicle theft, and arson). Less significant crimes are not included in the index. The index is widely publicized and is regarded as a crime report card. When the crime rate goes down, elected officials tout their success. When the crime index goes up, the politicians are criticized by their rivals. The politicians, in turn, put pressure on their police chiefs to reduce the crime rate, who in turn put pressure on those below them in the police hierarchy.

All of this creates tremendous temptations to demonstrate progress in reducing crime by massaging the figures. As one Chicago detective explained,

"It's so easy." First, the responding officer can intentionally misclassify a case or alter the narrative to record a lesser charge. A house break-in becomes "trespassing"; a garage break-in becomes "criminal damage to property"; a theft becomes "lost property."[4]

In each of these cases, what had been a major offense becomes a minor crime, not reflected in the FBI Uniform Crime Report. The temptations to understate crimes is sufficiently great that the New York Police Department devotes substantial resources to auditing the reports it receives, and to punishing officers found to have misreported.[5] But not every police force has the resources—or the will—to create these countervailing forces.

Nor is the problem confined to the United States. In London, England, the Mayor's Office for Policing and Crime set as a performance target a 20 percent reduction in crime. The target was passed down the chain of command, from the police commissioner to the constables on the beat, whose chances for promotion were linked to hitting the 20 percent target. In 2013, a whistle-blower from the London police force told a parliamentary committee that massaging statistics had become "an ingrained part of policing culture": serious crimes such as robbery were downgraded to "theft snatch," and rapes were often underreported so as to hit performance targets. As a retired detective chief superintendent put it, "When targets are set by offices such as the Mayor's Office for Policing and Crime, what they think they are asking for are 20% fewer victims. That translates into 'record 20% fewer crimes' as far as . . . senior officers are concerned." Such underreporting and downgrading of crimes "are common knowledge at every level in every police force within England and Wales," he added. Other experts explained the various techniques for improving the performance metrics: choosing not to believe complainants; recording multiple incidents in the same area as a single crime; and downgrading incidents to less serious crimes.[6]

Another temptation is perhaps more troubling still. It involves an additional key metric of police success: arrest statistics as a purported measure of effectiveness. Ed Burns, a former Baltimore police detective for the homicide and narcotics divisions—best known as co-creator of the HBO series *The Wire*—has described the process of "juking the stats," by which police officials could orient the activity of the department toward seemingly impressive outcomes. As a detective in the narcotics division, Burns sought to meticulously build a case against top drug lords. But his superiors were uninterested in that prospect, which was consuming manpower and would take years to produce an arrest. They were interested in enhancing the metrics, and since arresting five teenagers a day selling drugs on street corners yielded better statistics than arresting a drug king-pin after a multiyear investigation, they favored the course that quickly produced the higher numbers. From their point of view—and from the point of view of the politicians to whom they reported—every arrest was of the same value. The course of action that produced the best performance indicators did little to diminish the sale of narcotics.[7] When every unit is of equal weight, the temptation is to go after the easiest cases.[8] In Britain, this process of directing police resources at easier-to-solve crimes in order to boost detection rates is known as "skewing."

Metrics, then, have played a useful role in policing. But the attempt to use metrics as a basis of reward and punishment can lead to metrics that are less reliable and even counterproductive.

THE MILITARY

The U.S. military is perhaps the largest and most complex organization in the world. And since at least the Vietnam era, it has tried to use metrics in its counterinsurgency (COIN) campaigns, most recently in Iraq and Afghanistan. Though a small part of the U.S. military's use of metrics, COIN is a particularly instructive case, with larger ramifications for our topic. For not only has the military made extensive use of metrics in the interests of accountability and transparency, its efforts have also been scrutinized by academic researchers working at American military academies and at the Rand Corporation, which conducts research for the Department of Defense. Some of these researchers are both soldiers and scholars, while others have a more conventional academic background. What characterizes their work is close contact with actual experience, either in the form of direct participation in counterinsurgency or of access to recently deployed officers. Writing in good part for policymakers and officers who will be deployed in the future, the stakes of their scholarship are high. As a result, perhaps, some are extraordinarily honest and astute about the use and misuse of metrics.[1]

As the American experience in Vietnam shows, metrics may be misleading, and their pursuit may have unseen negative consequences. For one thing, the information may be costly to gather: American soldiers lost their lives searching for corpses to include in the body counts so valued by Secretary of Defense McNamara (see chapter 3). Those statistics were frequently exaggerated in order to boost the commanding officers' chances of promotion. And the stream of seemingly objective but actually fallacious information led policymakers and politicians to mistake improvement in the measured performance for real progress.[2]

David Kilcullen is a soldier/scholar who served as an officer in the Australian army before moving to the United States. He has held a number of key positions as a strategist of counterinsurgency for the U.S. Army and the Department of State, and spent time in Afghanistan and Iraq. His book *Counterinsurgency* includes an illuminating essay, "Measuring Progress in Afghanistan." "Counterinsurgency," as he simply puts it, is "whatever governments do to defeat rebellions."[3] The environment faced by counterinsurgents is complex and dynamic: "Insurgents and terrorists evolve rapidly in response to countermeasures, so that what works once may not work again, and insights that are valid for one area or one period may not apply elsewhere." Thus, Kilcullen emphasizes, metrics must be adapted to the particularities of the case: standardized metrics drawn from past wars in other venues will simply not work. Not only that, but use of the best performance metrics demands judgment based upon experience:

> Interpretation of indicators is critically important, and requires informed expert judgment. It is not enough merely to count incidents or conduct quantitative or statistical analysis—interpretation is a qualitative activity based on familiarity with the environment, and it needs to be conducted by experienced personnel who have worked in that environment for long enough to detect trends by comparison with previous conditions. These trends may not be obvious to personnel who are on short-duration tours in country, for example.[4]

Kilcullen explains why many standard metrics can be deceptive and should be avoided, including body counts and counts
of "significant activity" (SIGACTs), meaning violent incidents
against counterinsurgency forces. The usual assumption is
that the lower the number of such violent encounters, the
better. But that is not necessarily the case, Kilcullen explains,
since "[v]iolence tends to be high in contested areas and low
in government-controlled areas. But it is also low in enemy-
controlled areas, so that a low level of violence indicates that
someone is fully in control of a district but does not tell us
who." He also warns against the use of all "input metrics," that
is, metrics that count what the army and its allies are doing,
for these may be quite distinct from the *outcomes* of those
actions:

> Input metrics are indicators based on our own level of
> effort, as distinct from the effects of our efforts. For ex-
> ample, input metrics include numbers of enemy killed,
> numbers of friendly forces trained, numbers of schools or
> clinics built, miles of road completed, and so on. These
> indicators tell us what we are doing but not the effect we
> are having. To understand that effect, we need to look at
> output metrics (how many friendly forces are still serving
> three months after training, for example, or how many
> schools or clinics are still standing and in use after a year)
> or, better still, at outcome metrics. Outcome metrics track
> the actual and perceived effect of our actions on the popu-
> lation's safety, security, and well-being.[5]

Coming up with useful metrics often requires an immer-
sion in local conditions. Take, for example, the market price
of exotic (i.e., nonlocal) vegetables, which few outsiders look
to as a useful indicator of a population's perceived peace and

well-being. Kilcullen, however, explains why they might be helpful:

> Afghanistan is an agricultural economy, and crop diversity varies markedly across the country. Given the free-market economics of agricultural production in Afghanistan, risk and cost factors—the opportunity cost of growing a crop, the risk of transporting it across insecure roads, the risk of selling it at market and of transporting money home again—tend to be automatically priced in to the cost of fruits and vegetables. Thus, fluctuations in overall market prices may be a surrogate metric for general popular confidence and perceived security. In particular, exotic vegetables—those grown outside a particular district that have to be transported further at greater risk in order to be sold in that district—can be a useful telltale marker.[6]

Thus, *developing* valid metrics of success and failure requires a good deal of local knowledge, knowledge that may be of no use in other circumstances—to the chagrin of those who look for universal templates and formulae. The hard part is knowing *what* to count, and what the numbers you have counted actually *mean* in context.

Some broader lessons of counterinsurgency assessment are drawn out by Ben Connable, an analyst at the Rand Corporation, in his recent study *Embracing the Fog of War: Assessment and Metrics in Counterinsurgency.* "It would be difficult (if not impossible)," he writes, "to develop a practical, centralized model for COIN assessment because complex COIN environments cannot be clearly interpreted through a centralized process that removes data from their salient local context." Therefore "information can have very different meanings from place to place and over time." The problem arises from "the incongruity between decentralized and complex COIN operations and centralized, decontextualized assessment."[7]

These concerns apply well beyond the military realm: to the extent that we try to develop performance metrics for *any* complex environment or organization that is either unique or substantially different from other environments or organizations, standardized measures of performance will be inaccurate and deceptive. Yet the desire to create performance metrics that are "transparent" in the interests of "accountability" usually translates into using metrics that are standardized and centralized, since such metrics are more easily grasped by superiors and by publics far from the field of operations. Moreover, as another recent Rand study notes, observations that are communicated through quantitative measures are regarded as "empirical," while observations conveyed in qualitative form are treated as less reliable, despite the fact that "in practice, many of the quantitative metrics used in assessments are themselves anecdotal in that they reflect the observational bias of those reporting."[8]

Connable characterizes counterinsurgency as "both art and science, but mostly art."[9] That applies to the management of many other complex situations. The tendency is to treat as pure, measureable science what is of necessity largely a matter of art, requiring judgment based on experience.

BUSINESS AND FINANCE

WHEN PAYING FOR PERFORMANCE WORKS, AND WHEN IT DOESN'T

"But surely," you might think, "there is a place where pay for measured performance is appropriate, and that is in the realm of business." Businesses, after all, exist to make money, and people work in them to make money for themselves. It makes sense, it seems, for business managers to try to elicit their employees' greatest effort by tying their remuneration as closely as possible to their measurable contribution to making profits for the firm.

There are indeed circumstances when pay for measured performance fulfills that promise: when the work to be done is repetitive, uncreative, and involves the production or sale of standardized commodities or services; when there is little possibility of exercising choice over what one does; when there is little intrinsic satisfaction in it; when performance is based almost exclusively on individual effort, rather than that of a team; and when aiding, encouraging, and mentoring others is not an important part of the job. For sales forces,[1] or for routinized, individualized, highly focused jobs involving standardized outputs and without broader responsibilities, rewarding measured performance may well pay off. In short, as one sociologist has put it, "Extrinsic rewards become an important determinant of job satisfaction only among workers for whom intrinsic rewards are relatively unavailable."[2] These are the sort of tasks for which Taylorism (see chapter 3) was designed. There are many such jobs in any society, including a modern, technologically advanced one. But in our time, as the technologies of robotics and artificial intelligence advance, such jobs are becoming fewer and far between.[3]

But the salient fact is that most private-sector jobs do *not* match these criteria. And to the extent that they do not, direct payment for measured performance will be inappropriate and perhaps counterproductive.

People *do* want to be rewarded for their performance, both in terms of recognition and remuneration. But there is a difference between promotions (and raises) based on a range of qualities, and direct remuneration based on measured quantities of output. For most workers, contributions to their company include many activities that are intangible but no less real: coming up with new ideas and better ways to do things, exchanging ideas and resources with colleagues, engaging in teamwork, mentoring subordinates, relating to suppliers or customers, and more. It's appropriate to reward such activities through promotions and bonuses—even if it is more difficult to document and requires a greater degree of judgment by those who decide on the rewards. Nor is the problem assigning numbers to performance. There is nothing wrong with rating people on a scale. The problems arise when the scale is too one-dimensional, measuring only a few outputs that are most easily measured because they can be standardized.

Indeed, the academic evidence on pay for the measured performance of CEOs and other personnel is sufficiently troubling that some scholars of organizational behavior have suggested that it should simply be eliminated. And some companies are acting accordingly. Dan Cable and Freek Vermeulen of the London Business School recall many of the problems we have explored: the depressive effect of performance pay on creativity; the propensity to cook the books; the inevitable imperfections of the measurement instruments; the difficulty of defining long-term performance; and the tendency for extrinsic motivation to crowd out intrinsic motivation. They've concluded that it might be more advantageous to abolish pay-for-performance for top managers, and replace it with a higher fixed salary. They even suggest, rather heretically, that you might not want people motivated primarily by extrinsic motivation at the head of your company: yet the more compensation is variable and linked to measured performance, the more likely that that will be precisely the sort of people you will get.[4] And at least one of Britain's best-known investors, Neil Woodford of Woodford Investment Management, a company with £14.3 billion under management, has eliminated bonuses for the company's executives in favor of higher fixed pay, arguing that there is little correlation between bonus and performance.[5]

Forced ranking, in which managers are instructed to evaluate their employees compared to fellow employees, is another manifestation of metric fixation. It seems "hard" and "objective," but often turns out to be counterproductive. A 2006 survey of more than two hundred human resource professionals from large companies found that "even though over half of the companies used forced ranking, the respondents reported that this approach resulted in lower productivity, inequity, skepticism, decreased employee engagement, reduced collaboration, damage to morale, and mistrust in leadership."[6]

Increasing numbers of technology companies, conscious of the demotivating effect of performance rankings on the majority of their staff, are moving away from performance bonuses. They are replacing them with higher base salaries combined with shares or share options, to give employees a tangible interest in the long-term flourishing of the company (while paying special rewards to particularly high performers).[7]

Yet other companies are dropping annual ratings in favor of "crowdsourced" continuous performance data, by which supervisors, colleagues, and internal customers provide ongoing online feedback about employee performance. That may be substituting the frying pan for the fire, as employees constantly game for compliments, while resenting the omnipresent surveillance of their activities[8]—a dystopian possibility captured in Dave Eggers 2014 novel *The Circle*. Yet as improvements in information technology make it easier to monitor one or another index of worker performance, it will become ever more tempting to link pay to performance, whether in the form of piece rates, bonuses, or commissions[9]—in spite of evidence of the hazards of measuring too narrowly, and of discouraging teamwork and innovation.

A great deal of corporate dysfunction comes from pay-for-performance schemes that are narrowly tailored to measure a single outcome. Problems occur both at the top and at the bottom of the corporate ladder.

For a dramatic instance among top executives, take the case of the pharmaceutical manufacturer Mylan. Though not among the largest of American pharmaceutical firms (11th by revenue and 16th by market capitalization), it had the second-highest level of executive compensation: over the course of five years ending in December 2015, its top three managers were paid over $70,000,000 each. Over that period, its stock price rose 155 percent. In 2014 its board of directors developed a compensation scheme for the company's top executives according to which they would be handsomely rewarded if the company's profits grew by 16 percent each year—far beyond reasonable expectations for a company that dealt largely in generic drugs, generally considered a "mature market" where high rates of competition make for modest profits.

Mylan's largest profit center was the EpiPen, a penlike device that easily injects epinephrine (adrenalin) into the skin to counteract severe allergic shock. Because each injection lasts for only a brief time, and because children at risk of allergic shock require a pen at home and at school, many families with a member at risk need to stock several pens at once. Since the medicine loses its potency after 12 to 18 months, the pens need to be replaced frequently. Mylan did not create the EpiPen: it was developed by another company that brought it to market in 1987. Mylan bought the rights in 2007; but since there was no effective competitor in the market, it had a near monopoly on epinephrine injectors.

In 2011, Mylan promoted one of its top executives, Heather Bresch, to the position of Chief Executive Officer, effective January 2012. From 2009 to 2013, the company upped the list price of a two-pen pack from $100 to $263; then in May 2014 (just as the new incentive system for its top executives kicked in), it doubled the price to $461, before hiking it again in May 2015, to $608.[10]

By the summer of 2016, Mylan's price gouging on this essential device—used not only by many adults but also (thanks to a marketing campaign by Mylan) by thousands of school-age children—led to a public outcry and a congressional hearing. Several senators asked the Department of Justice to investigate the company's billing practices.

How did Mylan investors fare from the company's drive to incentivize its executives to raise profits? When Bresch took charge as CEO, the stock price stood at $22. In June 2015 it reached a high of $73. But the public outcry against the company and the resulting congressional hearings and Justice Department investigations led the price to drop to $36 in October 2016. The top executives' single-minded focus on hitting outsized profit metrics had led to a collapse of the company's reputation.

At the very time that Mylan's pay-for-performance scheme for top executives was bringing down the pharmaceutical company, another major corporation was being laid low by its own version of pay-for-performance. The company in question aimed not at the top of the organizational ladder but at the bottom; its incentives were not the carrots of monetary rewards but the sticks of forced termination for those who did not measure up to its performance goals.

Here's what happened. Wells Fargo, a major American bank, was functioning in a difficult economic environment. The Federal Reserve Board had lowered the rate of interest almost to the vanishing point, making it more difficult for banks to generate profits from the loans they extended. In an attempt to increase its profits, in 2011 the company encouraged "cross-selling": it set quotas for its employees to sign up customers who were interested in one of its products (say, a deposit account) for additional services, such as overdraft coverage or credit cards, which were more lucrative for the bank. Failure to reach the quota meant working additional hours without pay and the threat of termination. (Perhaps their inspiration was the Alex Baldwin character in the film *Glengarry Glen Ross*, a boss who instructs his sales force on the rules of their sales tournament: "First prize is a Cadillac El Dorado. . . . Second prize is a set of steak knives. Third prize is you're fired. Get the picture?") But the quotas were set too high, given the limited number of customers who entered the bank on a daily basis. To reach their enrollment quotas, thousands of Wells Fargo bankers resorted to low-level fraud, creating PIN numbers to enroll customers in online accounts or debit cards, for example—without informing the customer. That was not the intention of the Wells Fargo management: they wanted their employees to get customers to open legitimate accounts. As it uncovered evidence of malfeasance, Wells Fargo fired some 5,300 employees for their actions. But the spate of fraud was a predictable response to the performance quotas that the company's managers had set for their employees.

After news of the massive fraud broke in September 2016, Wells Fargo was fined $100,000,000 by the federal Consumer Financial Protection Bureau, $50,000,000 by the Los Angeles City Attorney, and $35,000,000 by the Office of the Controller of the Currency. The damage to the firm was not only monetary but also reputational. The value of Wells Fargo stock fell from about $50 in late August to $43 by the end of September. Once again, reward and punishment for measured performance backfired.[11]

The cases of Mylan and Wells Fargo are recent examples of an older and common pattern, by which policies of payment for measured performance lead employees to engage in actions that create long-run damage to a firm's reputation.[12]

Is this a problem of human nature or of the propagation of the credo of paying for measured performance? To put it another way: is the notion of narrowly self-interested agents a fact of life, or is it exacerbated by a managerial ideology that uses extrinsic rewards based upon simple models of human behavior that then become self-fulfilling prophecies? Sometimes, the way in which managers and employees are addressed by their company actually influences the way they think, so that they come to act in the narrowly self-interested way posited by the most reductive versions of principal-agent theory, with deceit and guile.[13] In fact, it may create a situation in which the managers and employees most knowledgeable about the workings of the performance indicators are best positioned to manipulate those indicators for their own benefit, and most likely to do so.[14] Take, for example, the cases of Dennis Kozlowski, the CEO of Tyco; Bernard Ebbers, CEO of WorldCom; John Rigas, CEO of Adelphia: all went to prison in the early 2000s for enriching themselves by using their detailed knowledge of their firms' transactions to manipulate the performance measures through which they were compensated.[15]

The reaction to these scandals led to the passage of the Sarbanes-Oxley Act of 2002, which sought to strengthen corporate accountability, in part by holding the members of the board of directors of public corporations legally liable for the accuracy of financial statements. While complying with the act has added substantial costs to the corporations, it may have strengthened public confidence in the validity of their financial reports—and so provides evidence of the advantages of transparency. But the increased legal accountability of each member of the board of directors has also imposed costs of a sort not measureable by economists. As a consultant to the boards of directors of Fortune 500 corporations (who for obvious reasons must remain nameless) told me, since the passage of Sarbanes-Oxley, board members are so focused on assuring the accuracy of the company's financial reports that they have little time and inclination to deliberate upon the primary tasks of a board of directors, namely thinking strategically about the long-range future of the company! Thus *only* what gets measured—and potentially penalized—gets done.

THE FINANCIAL CRISIS

The financial crisis of 2008 had many causes, and some of them flowed from the attempt to substitute standardized metrics for judgment based on local knowledge, exacerbated by the effects of pay-for-performance schemes.[16]

As companies, including financial companies, grew larger and more diverse in their holdings, new layers of management were needed to supervise and coordinate their disparate units. From the point of view of top management, the diversity of operations meant that executives were managing assets with which they had little familiarity. That led to a search for standardized measures of performance across large and disparate organizations. Its implicit premises were these: that information which is numerically measurable is the only sort of knowledge necessary; that numerical data can substitute for other forms of inquiry; and that numerical acumen (premised upon probabilistic formulas rather than empirical research) can substitute for practical knowledge about the underlying assets.

Contributing to the financial crisis was the increasing role of financial managers who were skilled at the analysis and manipulation of metric data but did not have "concrete" knowledge or experience of the things being made or traded. As Niall Ferguson has put it, "those whom the gods want to destroy they first teach math."

Here, in stylized form, is what happened in the lead-up to the crisis of 2008. Traditionally, banks (or individual investors) had offered mortgages to people with whom they had direct contact. They were thus in a position to exercise judgment about who was credit-worthy and who was not. And they had an incentive to exercise that judgment: since the bank (or investor) continued to hold the mortgage, their stream of future income depended on the reliability of the mortgagee.

That began to change around the year 2000, and by 2008 that system had largely been replaced by a new one. Changes in the capital regulations of banks made the origination and holding of traditional mortgages less lucrative than holding securities comprising thousands of mortgages.[17] Now the mortgages were originated not by the bank but by a mortgage brokerage firm, which made its money from the number of mortgages it processed but had no financial interest in the long-term viability of the mortgages. Mortgage originators, such as Countrywide, provided loans to people buying houses, then packaged these loans into bundles of one thousand, and sold them to a bank, such as Lehman Brothers. Since they had no long-term interest in the viability of the mortgage loans they issued, mortgage originators increasingly offered "low-doc" or "no-doc" loans, meaning that borrowers were asked to provide almost no proof that they would actually be able to repay the loans. But the bank did not hold onto them either. It created a "mortgage backed security," an interest-bearing bond, secured by the loans, and sold these to investors. With advice from the ratings agencies (such as Moody's), financial engineers mixed good-quality mortgages, from borrowers likely to pay, with more dubious ones, so as to squeeze the most profit out of these mortgage-backed securities,[18] which they carved into "tranches" bearing different degrees of risk in return for varying rates of interest. Behind all of this was a belief in the financial sector that such diversification was a substitute for due diligence on each asset. The idea was that if one bundled enough assets together, one didn't have to know much about the assets, or make judgments about their viability.

New, mathematically complex financial instruments were created, such as credit default swaps, which were intended to insure against the risk of sudden changes in the value of mortgage-backed securities. This was supposed to use mathematical sophistication to diminish risk, but instead led to an inability of any but a few analysts to get a clear sense of what was happening. And the creation of arcane financial instruments made effective supervision virtually impossible, both by superiors in the firm and by outside regulators.

Add to this witches' brew of dubious metrics, served up as a replacement for judgment, the fact that the remuneration of top employees at banks such as Lehman Brothers was based on pay for measured performance in the form of bonuses. Thus metrics provided the means, and .pay-for-performance supplied the motivation, for undue risk-taking under conditions of opacity.[19] Then, as mortgagees proved unable to make their mortgage payments, the simultaneous drop in value of mortgage-backed securities led to huge, unanticipated losses to those financial firms that had insured the securities through credit default swaps. The result was a near meltdown of the financial system.

SHORT-TERMISM

Another way in which dubious indicators of measured performance have distorted the economy is through short-termism.

Perhaps the most consequential change in the business world in recent decades has been the financialization of the economy, above all in the United States.[20] As late as the 1980s, finance was an essential but limited element of the American economy. Trade in equities (the stock market) was made up of individual investors, large and small, putting their own money into stocks of companies they believed to have good long-term prospects. Investment capital was available from the major Wall Street investment banks (and their foreign counterparts), which were private partnerships in which the partners' own money was on the line. All this began to change as larger pools of capital (from pension funds, university endowments, and foreign investors) became available for investment and came to be deployed by professional money managers rather than the owners of the capital themselves. The result was a new financial system, characterized as "money manager capitalism" by the maverick economist Hyman Minsky, or "agency capitalism" by Alfred Rappaport, a business school professor.[21]

Spurred in part by these new opportunities, the traditional Wall Street investment banks transformed themselves into publicly traded corporations—that is to say, they too began to invest not just with their own funds but also with other peoples' money—and tied the bonuses of their partners and employees to annual profits. All this created a highly competitive financial system dominated by investment managers working with large pools of capital, paid for their supposed ability to outperform their peers. The structure of incentives in this environment leads fund managers to try to maximize short-term returns, and they in turn pressure the executives of the corporations whose stock they own to show gains every quarter.[22]

The shrunken time horizon creates a temptation to boost immediate profits at the expense of longer-term investments, whether in research and development or in improving the skills of the company's workforce. The emphasis placed upon quarterly earnings (which are supposed to provide transparency) and "quarterly earnings guidance"—projections by management about the firm's profitability in the coming three months—intensifies short-termism, since stock prices often rise and fall in keeping with this metric. And since the failure to reach this predicted target by the end of the next quarter may also lead to declines in stock prices, there is an inescapable temptation to game the figures so that measured performance matches the projections. It creates tremendous incentives for corporate executives to devote their creative energies to schemes that demonstrate productivity or profit by massaging the data, or by underinvesting in maintenance and human capital formation (ongoing education of employees) to boost quarterly earnings or their equivalents. The propensity for underinvestment in long-term growth is sufficiently dire that in early 2016, the CEO of the largest investment firm in the world, Larry Fink of BlackRock, wrote an open letter in which he warned, "Today's culture of quarterly earnings hysteria is totally contrary to the long-term approach that we need."[23]

Gaming the metrics often takes the form of diverting resources away from their best long-term uses to achieve measured short-term goals. Take the company that, hoping to be bought out at a multiple of earnings, tries to boost its profit by laying off necessary workers. Or the CEO who smooths out corporate earnings by postponing needed investments in an effort to meet analysts' expectations for the quarter. Or the money-managers who buy shares of well-performing stocks and sell shares of underperforming stocks in time for listing in quarterly reports, disguising the fact that they bought the high-performing stocks at high prices and that their poorly-performing stocks may have turned around had they held onto them—known in the trade as "window dressing."[24]

A focus on measurable performance indicators can lead managers to neglect tasks for which no clear measures of performance are available, as the organizational scholars Nelson Repenning and Rebecca Henderson have recently noted.[25] Unable to count intangible assets such as reputation, employee satisfaction, motivation, loyalty, trust, and cooperation, those enamored of performance metrics squeeze assets in the short term at the expense of long-term consequences. For all these reasons, reliance upon measurable metrics is conducive to short-termism, a besetting malady of contemporary American corporations.

OTHER DYSFUNCTIONS

When rewards such as pay, bonuses, and promotions are tied to meeting budget targets, there is yet another danger: distorting the information system of the organization. Managers and employees learn to lie, to massage, embellish, or disguise the numbers that are used to calculate their pay. But since these are the very numbers that executives use to coordinate the activities of the organization and decide on the allocation of future resources, the productivity and efficiency of the organization is damaged as resources are misallocated.[26]

The attempt to substitute precise measurement for informed judgment also limits innovation, which necessarily entails guesswork and risk. As business school professors Gary Pisano and Willy Shih have argued,

> Most companies are wedded to highly analytical methods for evaluating investment opportunities. Still, it remains

enormously hard to assess long-term R&D programs with quantitative techniques. . . . Usually, the data, or even reasonable estimates, are simply not available. Nonetheless, all too often these tools become the ultimate arbiter of what gets funded and what does not. So short-term projects with more predictable outcomes beat out the long-term investments needed to replenish technical and operating capabilities.[27]

Performance metrics as a measure of accountability help to allocate blame when things go badly, but do little to encourage success,[28] especially when success requires imagination, innovation, and risk. Indeed, as the economist Frank Knight noted almost a century ago, entrepreneurship entails "immeasureable uncertainty," which is not susceptible to metric calculation.[29]

Thus, even in business and finance, metric fixation takes its toll. Businesses must be judged by more than one indicator of performance. Profit surely matters. But so, in the long run, does reputation, market share, customer satisfaction, and employee morale, which makes it possible to adapt and to find solutions to the new problems that will inevitably arise in the marketplace. In an economic world characterized by unpredictable change, there is a need for ongoing innovation, small and large, that is not readily reducible to a single performance target. Performance indicators can certainly aid, but not replace, the key functions of management: thinking ahead, judging, and deciding.[30]

PHILANTHROPY AND FOREIGN AID

As we've seen, performance metrics readily become dysfunctional in governmental settings and in profit-making businesses, and that holds true for nonprofit organizations as well. As in the previous case studies, our purpose is not to survey the field as a whole but to offer some exemplary instances.

Like corporations and government agencies, charities are under pressure to be transparent in their workings and accountable to their donors, and it is often thought that the surest way to do so is by the use of performance metrics. Donors are presumed to want their contributions to be used efficiently, and for the stated goals of the nonprofit organizations to which they contribute. But how is that to be evaluated? And how are they to ensure that the funds are not siphoned off primarily for the benefit of the charity's staff?

In recent decades, under the spell of metric fixation, funders—foundations, governments, and individuals—decided that the solution was to measure and publicize the percentage of each charity's budget that was devoted to administrative and fund-raising costs ("overhead" or "indirect expenses") as opposed to its activities or programs. Once again we see a pattern that we've encountered in regard to the use of metrics. What gets measured is what is most easily measured, and since the outcomes of charitable organizations are more difficult to measure than their inputs, it is the inputs that get the attention. At the extremes, the ratio of overhead-to-program costs can provide a useful indicator of fraud or of poor financial management. But too often, measured performance that may be useful in aberrant cases is extended to all cases.

For most charities, equating low overhead with higher productivity is not only deceptive but downright counterproductive. In order to be successful, charitable organizations need competent, trained staff. They need adequate computer and information systems. They need functional offices. And yes, the ability to keep raising funds. But the assumption that the effectiveness of charities is inversely proportional to their overhead expenses leads to underspending on overhead and the degradation of organizational capacities: instead of high-quality and well-trained staff, too many novices and too much staff turnover; computer systems that are out of date and inefficient; and as a result, less effectiveness in raising funds for ongoing activities or new programs. To make matters worse, the funders impose growing demands for reports, so that staff time devoted to documentation eats up an ever larger portion of the grant.

In response, the leaders of charitable organizations often end up trying to game the figures: by reporting that the time of leading staff members is devoted almost entirely to programs, or that there is no spending on fundraising. That response is understandable. But it feeds the expectations of funders that low overhead is the measure they should be looking at to hold charities accountable.[1] Thus the snake of accountability eats its own tail.

THE TRANSFORMATIONAL VERSUS THE MEASUREABLE

Metric fixation is also evident in government foreign aid intended to promote social and economic development. There is a deeply ingrained and partly well-founded skepticism about foreign aid, which has too often been unproductive and indeed counterproductive.[2] But some foreign aid programs do genuinely contribute to the health, education, economic development, and even political stability of poor countries. In trying to measure what works and what doesn't, American government agencies have increasingly looked to metrics, with results that might by now be predictable to readers of this book.

Programs whose achievements are not easily measured in quantitative terms have been curtailed. It is easier to measure enrollment in primary schools and literacy rates, for example, than the sort of cultural education of future elites that comes from providing scholarships for students from poor countries to study in American universities. So when metrics becomes the standard of evaluation, programs that cannot demonstrate their short-term benefits are sacrificed. The U.S. Agency for International Development's scholarship program, for example, was gutted by the White House Office of Management and Budget on the grounds that its benefits could not be put into dollar terms, and thus the government could not determine whether the program's benefits exceeded its costs.[3]

Here, too, metrics promotes short-termism. Andrew Natsios, a distinguished public servant with long experience in international development, notes that the employees of government agencies in this field have "become infected with a very bad case of Obsessive Measurement Disorder, an intellectual dysfunction rooted in the notion that counting everything in government programs will produce better policy choices and improved management." The emphasis on quantification leads to a neglect of programs with the longest-run potential benefits: those that improve the skills, knowledge, and norms of the civil service and judicial systems in under-developed nations. Those who suffer from Obsessive Measurement Disorder, Natsios writes, ignore "a central principle of development theory—that those development programs that are most precisely and easily measured are the least transformational, and those programs that are the most transformational are the least measureable."[4] High among those are the development of competent leadership and management.

Here, too, the urge to measure the most easily measureable leads to a focus not on outcomes but on measureable inputs, such as bureaucratic processes. As a USAID official confessed to one scholar, "No one has come up with a valid way to quantify the effectiveness of capacity building activities. . . . So instead of focusing on effectiveness in reporting, USAID focuses on what can be measured, such as the number of workshops held or the number of people who have participated in training."[5]

The demand for more measurement and more quantification comes not only from congressional committees but also from executive agencies such as the Office of Management and Budget and from the Government Accountability Office, agencies staffed in good part by "accountants, economists, procurement officers, and legislative staffers who . . . bear the stamp of professors in public administration, business administration, or economics who overemphasized quantification in educating them."[6] These professional measurers are the vestal virgins of the sacred fire of metrics. They are also proselytizers, converting their senior management to the cult, which demands a substantial sacrifice of time and energy in the form of statistical reports with which to measure performance and ensure accountability.

EXCURSUS

WHEN TRANSPARENCY IS THE ENEMY OF PERFORMANCE

POLITICS, DIPLOMACY, INTELLIGENCE, AND MARRIAGE

The appeal of metrics is based in good part on the notion that institutions will be unresponsive if they are opaque, and more effective if they are subject to external monitoring. Google's Ngram viewer shows a steep ascent in the mid-1980s for both "performance metrics" and "transparency," with the two terms rising more or less in tandem. And it is characteristic of our culture that we tend to assume that performance and transparency rise and fall together. But that is a fallacy, or at least a misleading generalization. For just as there are limits to the efficacy of measured performance, there are limits to the efficacy of transparency. In some cases, how well our institutions perform depends on *not* making them transparent. At issue here is not the question of metrics, but of performance in the broadest sense: success in what we're supposed to be doing. To appreciate the dark side of transparency, let us begin not with organizations but with interpersonal relations.

INTIMACY

Our very sense of self is possible only because our thoughts and desires are *not* transparent to others. The possibility of intimacy depends on our ability to make ourselves more transparent to some people than to others. As the contemporary philosopher Moshe Halbertal puts it,

> If a person's thoughts were written on his forehead, exposed before all, the distinction between interior and exterior would vanish, and with it also individuation. Privacy, expressed through the possibility of concealment, thus protects the very ability of a person to define himself as an individual. Furthermore, the self may create special relationships by displaying differential measures of exposure and intimacy. He moves through social space by allotting revelation and concealment and establishing differential measures of distance and closeness.[1]

In interpersonal relations, even the most intimate ones, success depends on a degree of ambiguity and opacity, on *not* knowing everything that the other is doing, never mind thinking.

POLITICS AND GOVERNMENT

A certain degree of opacity is even more necessary when it comes to politics, where there are many more actors involved, and hence more interests and more sensibilities. One major role of politicians is to broker those diverse interests and sensibilities and to arrive at arrangements that bridge differences. This strategy entails negotiation, trading off some interests against others in an attempt to attain a compromise that will be tolerable to a number of interests, though rarely entirely satisfactory to any one of them. To put it another way, it involves the bargaining away of many positions, at least as defined by the interested parties. More often than not, that is possible only when the negotiation takes place protected from the view of the various claimants, each of whom might try to veto any compromise that struck at their publicly defined, "transparent" position. What politicians call "creative give and take," ideologues or representatives of special interests call "betrayal." That is why on sensitive matters, the negotiating process is most effective when it takes place behind closed doors. As Tom Daschle, the Democratic former majority leader of the Senate, has recently observed, the "idea that Washington would work better if there were TV cameras monitoring every conversation gets it exactly wrong.... The lack of opportunities for honest dialogue and creative give-and-take lies at the root of today's dysfunction."[2] That is also why effective politicians must to some degree be two-faced, pursuing more flexibility in closed negotiations than in their public advocacy. Only when multiple compromises have been made and a deal has been reached can it be subjected to public scrutiny, that is, made transparent.[3]

The same holds true for the performance of the government. Here, too, effective functioning often depends on not making internal deliberations open to the public—but rather on maintaining a lack of transparency. We need to distinguish between those elements of government that ought to be made public and those that should not be. Cass R. Sunstein, a wide-ranging academic who has also served in government, makes a useful distinction between government inputs and outputs. Outputs include data that the government produces on social and economic trends, as well as the results of government actions, such as regulatory rules. Outputs, he argues, ought to be made as publicly accessible as possible. Inputs, by contrast, are the discussions that go into government decision-making: discussions between policymakers and civil servants. There are increasing pressures to make those publicly available as well: whether through legal means such as Freedom of Information Act requests; or congressional demands, as in the case of congressional committees demanding the email correspondence of former Secretary of State Hillary Clinton in the case of the Benghazi investigations; or illegal means such as the electronic theft and dissemination of internal government documents by organizations such as Wikileaks. Making internal deliberations open to public disclosure—that is, transparent—is counterproductive, Sunstein argues, since if government officials know that all of their ideas and positions may be made public, it inhibits openness, candor, and trust in communications. The predictable result will be for government officials to commit ever less information to writing, either in print or in the form of emails. Instead, they will limit important matters to oral conversation. But that decreases the opportunity to carefully lay out positions.[4] All policies have costs: if internal deliberations are subject to transparency, it makes it impossible to deflate policy prescriptions that may be popular but are ill advised, or desirable but likely to offend one or another constituency. Thus transparency of inputs becomes the enemy of good government.

DIPLOMACY AND INTELLIGENCE

Transparency is also a hazard in diplomacy, and is fatal to the gathering of intelligence. In 2010, Bradley Manning, an intelligence analyst in the American Army, took it upon himself to disclose hundreds of thousands of sensitive military and State Department documents through WikiLeaks.[5] One result was the publication of the names of confidential informants, including political dissidents, who had spoken with American diplomats in Iran, China, Afghanistan, the Arab world, and elsewhere.[6] As a consequence, some of these individuals had to be relocated to protect their lives. More importantly, the revelations made it more difficult for American diplomats to acquire human intelligence in the future, since the confidentiality of conversations could not be relied upon.

Then, in 2013, Edward Snowden, a computer security specialist formerly employed by the CIA and more recently as a contractor for the NSA in Hawaii, systematically set out to copy thousands of highly secret documents from a variety of government agencies in order to expose the American government's surveillance programs. Among the many sensitive documents he made available to the press was the eighteen-page text of Presidential Policy Directive 20 on cyber operations, revealing every foreign computer system targeted for potential action—a document published in full by the British journal *The Guardian*. The release of documents stolen by Snowden and publicized by leading media outlets was not only the most significant breach of American intelligence ever, it also represented a powerful blow to the national security of the United States and its friends and allies. Yet Snowden was hailed as a hero by portions of the public in the United States and Europe. At the heart of the Snowden debacle lies the belief that transparency is always desirable.

A thriving polity, like a healthy marriage, relegates some matters to the shadows. In international relations, as in interpersonal ones, many practices are functional so long as they remain ambiguous and opaque. Clarity and publicity kill. The ability to negotiate between couples or states often involves coming up with formulas that allow each side to save face or retain self-esteem, and that requires compromising principles, or ambiguity. The fact that allies spy on one another to a certain degree to determine intentions, capacities, and vulnerabilities is well known to practitioners of government. But it cannot be publicly acknowledged, since it represents a threat to the amour propre of other nations. Moreover, in domestic politics and in international relations as in interpersonal ones, there is a role for a certain amount of hypocrisy for practices that are tolerable and useful but that can't be fully justified by international law and explicit norms.

In short, to quote Moshe Halbertal once again,

> A degree of legitimate concealment is necessary to maintain the state and its democratic institutions. Military secrets, techniques for fighting crime, intelligence gathering, and even diplomatic negotiations that will fall apart if they become exposed—all these domains have to stay shrouded in secrecy in order to allow the functioning of ordinary transparency in the other institutions of the state. Our transparent open conversation rests upon a rather extensive dark and hidden domain that insures its flourishing.[7]

We live in a world in which privacy is being eroded both through technology (the Internet) and a culture that proclaims the virtue of candor while dismissing the need for shame. In such a post-privacy society, people are inclined to overlook the value of secrecy.[8] Thus, the power of "transparency" as a magic formula is such that its counterproductive effects are often ignored. "Sunlight is the best disinfectant" has become the credo of the new faith of Wikileakism: the belief that making public the internal deliberations of all organizations and governments will make the world a better place.

But more often, the result is paralysis. Politicians forced to reveal their every action are unable to arrive at compromises that make legislation possible. Officials who need to fear that their internal deliberations will be made public are less positioned to make effective public policy. Intelligence agencies that require secrecy to gather information on the nation's enemies are thwarted. In each case, transparency becomes the enemy of performance.

IV

CONCLUSIONS

UNINTENDED BUT PREDICTABLE NEGATIVE CONSEQUENCES

One conception of the purpose of social science was articulated in the nineteenth century by Auguste Comte: *Savoir pour prévoir, prévoir pour prévenir* (Know in order to predict, predict in order to avert [the previously unanticipated consequences of our actions]). Now that we know a good deal about metric fixation, we can anticipate many of its unintended negative consequences, and perhaps avert them. Before we turn to the proper use of measured performance, let us gather together some lessons from our case studies about the recurrent perils of metrics.

Goal displacement through diversion of effort to what gets measured. Goal displacement comes in many varieties. When performance is judged by a few measures, and the stakes are high (keeping one's job, getting a raise, raising the stock price at the time that stock options are vested), people will focus on satisfying those measures—often at the expense of other, more important organizational goals that are not measured.[1] Economists Bengt Holmström and Paul Milgrom have described it in more formal terms as a problem of misaligned incentives: workers who are rewarded for the accomplishment of measurable tasks reduce the effort devoted to other tasks.[2] The result is that the metric *means* comes to replace the organizational *ends* that those means ought to serve.

Promoting short-termism. Measured performance encourages what Robert K. Merton called "the imperious immediacy of interests . . . where the actor's paramount concern with the foreseen immediate consequences excludes consideration of further or other consequences."[3] In short, advancing short-term goals at the expense of long-range considerations.

Costs in employee time. To the debit side of the ledger must also be added the transactional costs of metrics: the expenditure of employee time by those tasked with compiling and processing the metrics—not to speak of the time required to actually read them. That is exacerbated by the "reporting imperative"—the perceived need to constantly generate information, even when nothing significant is going on. Sometimes the metric of success is the number and size of the reports generated, as if nothing is accomplished unless it is extensively documented. Those within the organization end up spending more and more time compiling data, writing reports, and attending meetings at which the data and reports are coordinated. So, as the heterodox management consultants Yves Morieux and Peter Tollman note, employees work longer and harder at activities that add little to the real productiveness of their organization, while sapping their enthusiasm.[4]

Diminishing utility. Sometimes, newly introduced performance metrics will have immediate benefits in discovering poorly performing outliers.[5] Having gleaned the low-hanging fruit, there is tendency to expect a continuingly bountiful harvest. The problem is that the metrics continue to get collected from everyone. And soon the marginal costs of assembling and analyzing the metrics exceed the marginal benefits.

Rule cascades. In an attempt to staunch the flow of faulty metrics through gaming, cheating, and goal diversion, organizations institute a cascade of rules. Complying with them further slows down the institution's functioning and diminishes its efficiency.

Rewarding luck. Measuring outcomes when the people involved have little control over the results is tantamount to rewarding luck. It means that people are rewarded or penalized for outcomes that are actually independent of their efforts. Those penalized rightly feel that they've been treated unfairly.

Discouraging risk-taking. Attempts to measure productivity through performance metrics have other, more subtle effects: they not only promote short-termism, as noted earlier, but also discourage initiative and risk-taking. The intelligence analysts who ultimately located Bin Laden worked on the problem for years. If measured at any point, their productivity would have seemed to be zero. Month after month, their failure rate was 100 percent, until they achieved success. From the perspective of their superiors, allowing the analysts to work on the project for years involved a high degree of risk: the investment in time might not have panned out. Yet really great achievements often depend on such risks. This is typical of situations involving long-term investments of manpower.

Discouraging innovation. When people are judged by performance metrics, they are incentivized to do what the metrics measure, and what the metrics measure will be some established goal. But that impedes innovation, which means doing something that is not yet established, indeed hasn't been tried out. Innovation involves experimentation. Trying out something new entails risk, including the possibility, perhaps probability, of failure.[6] When performance metrics discourage risk they inadvertently promote stagnation.

Discouraging cooperation and common purpose. Rewarding individuals for measured performance diminishes the sense of common purpose as well as the social relationships that provide the unmeasureable motivation for cooperation and institutional effectiveness.[7] Reward based on measured performance tends to promote not cooperation but competition. If the individuals or units respond to the incentives created, rather than aiding, assisting, and advising one another, they strive to maximize their own metrics, ignoring, or even sabotaging, their fellows. As Donald Berwick, a leading medical reformer, has recounted,

> One hospital CEO described to me his system of profit-center management, in which middle management bonuses depended on local budget performance. I asked him if one of his managers would transfer resources from his department to another's if it would help the organization as a whole. "Yes," the CEO answered honestly, "if he were crazy."[8]

Degradation of work. Compelling the people in an organization to focus their efforts on the narrow range of what gets measured leads to a degradation of the experience of work. Edmund Phelps, a Nobel Prize winning economist, claims in his book *Mass Flourishing: How Grassroots Innovation Created Jobs, Challenge, and Change* that one of the virtues of capitalism is its ability to provide "the experience of mental stimulation, the challenge of new problems to solve, the chance to try the new, and the excitement of venturing into the unknown."[9] That is indeed a possibility under capitalism. But those subject to performance metrics are forced to focus their efforts on limited goals, imposed by others, who may not understand the work that they do. For the workers under scrutiny, mental stimulation is dulled, they decide neither the problems to be solved nor how to solve them, and there is no excitement of venturing into the unknown because the unknown is beyond the measureable. In short, the entrepreneurial element of human nature—which extends beyond the owners of enterprises—may be stifled by metric fixation.[10]

One result is to motivate those with greater initiative and enterprise to move out of mainstream, large-scale organizations where the culture of accountable performance prevails. Teachers move out of public schools to private schools and charter schools. Engineers move out of large corporations to boutique firms. Enterprising government employees become consultants. There is a healthy element in this. But surely the large-scale organizations of our society are the poorer for driving out those most likely to innovate and initiate. The more that work becomes a matter of filling in the boxes by which performance is to be measured and rewarded, the more it will repel those who think outside the box.

Costs to productivity. Economists who specialize in measuring economic productivity report that in recent years the only increase in total factor productivity in the American economy has been in the information-technology-producing industries.[11] A question that ought to be asked is to what extent the culture of metrics—with its costs in employee time, morale, and initiative, and its promotion of short-termism—has itself contributed to economic stagnation?

WHEN AND HOW TO USE METRICS

A CHECKLIST

There is nothing intrinsically pernicious about counting and measuring human performance. We all tend to project broad-ranging conclusions based on our inevitably limited experience, and measured data can serve as a useful counterpoint to those subjective judgments. The sort of measurements with which this book is concerned are performance metrics that quantify human achievement and failure. There are legitimate metrics of performance in almost every organization.

In our case studies, we've seen many instances in which metrics has been useful and effective.

In policing, computerized statistics of the incidence of crimes (Compstat) were used to good purpose, to discover where problems were greatest and where police resources were best deployed. It ran into problems only when officials used the threat of demotion or lack of promotion against those lower in the hierarchy to try to bring down the reported crime rates.

In universities, faculty evaluations can be enhanced by numerical data about publications and teaching. The metrics go awry when they are used mechanically by those who are not in a position to evaluate the accuracy and significance of the data.

In primary and secondary education, standardized tests can be used to inform teachers of how much or how little their students are learning in particular subjects. Teachers can consult with their colleagues, and adjust their methods and curriculum as a result. Problems arise when the tests become the primary basis on which teachers and schools are rewarded or punished.

In medicine, Peter Pronovost's Keystone project demonstrates how effective diagnostic metrics can be in lowering the incidence of medical errors, when what is measured accords with the professional values of practitioners. The success of the Geisinger medical system illustrates the remarkable improvements made possible by computerized measurement when integrated into an institutional culture based on cooperation, where the setting of measurement criteria and the evaluation of performance are done by teams that include physicians as well as administrators. In both cases, metrics were used in ways that appealed to intrinsic motivation and to professionalism. But elsewhere in the medical system, as we've seen, the use of reward for measured performance sometimes proved fruitless or led to perverse outcomes.

Reflections on the best use of performance metrics by the U.S. Army in its counterinsurgency campaigns showed that while standardized metrics are often deceptive, metrics developed to fit the specific case, especially by practitioners with local experience, could be genuinely informative. The challenge in such cases is to abandon universal templates and discover what is worth counting, and what the numbers actually mean in their local context.

As we've seen time and again, measurement is not an alternative to judgment: measurement *demands* judgment: judgment about whether to measure, what to measure, how to evaluate the significance of what's been measured, whether rewards and penalties will be attached to the results, and to whom to make the measurements available.

Should you find yourself in a position to set policy, here are the questions you should ask, and the factors you should keep in mind, in considering *whether* to use measured performance, and if so, *how* to use it. They constitute a checklist of successful performance measurement. Given what we've said about the hazards of metric fixation, consider at every point that the best use of metrics may be not to use it at all.

THE CHECKLIST

1. What *kind* of information are you thinking of measuring? The more the object to be measured resembles inanimate matter, the more likely it is to be measureable: that is why measurement is indispensable in the natural sciences and in engineering. When the objects to be measured are influenced by the process of measurement, measurement becomes less reliable. Measurement becomes much less reliable the more its object is human activity, since the objects—people—are self-conscious, and are capable of reacting to the process of being measured. And if rewards and punishments are involved, they are more likely to react in a way that skews the measurement's validity. By contrast, the more they agree with the goals of those rewards, the more likely they are to react in a way that enhances the measurement's validity.

2. How *useful* is the information? Always begin by reminding yourself that the fact that some activity is measureable does not make it worth measuring, indeed, the ease of measuring may be inversely proportional to the significance of what is measured. To put it another way, ask your-

self, is what you are measuring a proxy for what you really want to know? If the information is not very useful or not a good proxy for what you're really aiming at, you're probably better off not measuring it.

3. How useful are *more* metrics? Remember that measured performance, when useful, is more effective in identifying outliers, especially poor performers or true misconduct. It is likely to be less useful in distinguishing between those in the middle or near the top of the ladder of performance. Plus, the more you measure, the greater the likelihood that the marginal costs of measuring will exceed the benefits. So, the fact that metrics is helpful doesn't mean that more metrics is more helpful.

4. What are the costs of *not* relying upon standardized measurement? Are there other sources of information about performance, based on the judgment and experience of clients, patients, or parents of students? In a school setting, for example, the degree to which parents request a particular teacher for their children is probably a useful indicator that the teacher is doing something right, whether or not the results show up on standardized tests. In the case of charities, it may be most useful to allow the beneficiaries to judge the results.

5. To what *purposes* will the measurement be put, or to put it another way, to *whom* will the information be made transparent? Here a key distinction is between data to be used for purposes of internal monitoring of performance by the practitioners themselves versus data to be used by external parties for reward and punishment. For example, is crime data being used to discover where the police ought to deploy more squad cars or to decide whether the precinct commander will get a promotion? Or is a surgical

team using data to discover which procedures have worked best or are administrators using that same data to decide whether the hospital will be financially rewarded or penalized for its scores? Measurement instruments, such as tests, are invaluable, but they are most useful for internal analysis by practitioners rather than for external evaluation by public audiences who may fail to understand their limits. Such measurement can be used to inform practitioners of their performance relative to their peers, offering recognition to those who have excelled and offering assistance to those who have fallen behind. To the extent that they are used to determine continuing employment and pay, they will be subject to gaming the statistics or to outright fraud.

Remember that, as we've seen, performance metrics that link reward and punishment may actually help reinforce intrinsic motivation when the goals to be rewarded accord with the professional goals of the practitioners.[1] If, on the other hand, the scheme of reward and punishment is meant to elicit behavior that the practitioners consider useless or harmful, the metrics are more likely to be manipulated in the many ways we've explored. And if the practitioners are too geared toward extrinsic reward, they may well react by focusing their activity on what is measured and rewarded, at the expense of other facets of their work that may be equally important. For all these reasons, "low stakes" metrics are often more effective than when the stakes are higher.

Recall that direct pay-for-performance works best to the degree that people are motivated by extrinsic reward rather than intrinsic motivation, that is, when they care about making more money rather than about the other potential benefits of their work, social and intellectual.

That may be because they are in a field, such as finance, in which people measure their own vocational success almost entirely in terms of the amount they earn. (As we've noted, that doesn't preclude them from using their earnings for a wide range of purposes, including selfless ones.) It is when the job offers few other attractions—when it is repetitious and leaves little room for the exercise of choice, for example replacing windshields or preparing hamburgers—that pay for measured performance is more likely to work.

6. What are the *costs* of acquiring the metrics? Information is never free, and often it is expensive in ways that rarely occur to those who demand more of it. Collecting data, processing it, analyzing it—all of these take time, and their expense is in the opportunity costs of the time put into them. To put it another way, every moment you or your colleagues or employees are devoting to the production of metrics is time not devoted to the activities being measured. If you're a data analyst, of course, producing metrics *is* your primary activity. For everyone else, it's a distraction. So, even if the performance measurements are worth having, their worth may be less than the costs of obtaining them. Remember, too, that those costs in human time and effort are themselves almost impossible to calculate—another reason to err on the side of caution.

7. Ask why the people at the top of the organization are demanding performance metrics. As we've noted, the demand for performance measures sometimes flows from the ignorance of executives about the institutions they've been hired to manage, and that ignorance is often a result of parachuting into an organization with which one has little experience. Since experience and local knowledge

matter, lean toward hiring from within. Even if there is someone smarter and more successful elsewhere, their lack of particular knowledge of your company, university, government agency, or other organization may not outweigh the benefits of hiring from within.

8. *How* and *by whom* are the measures of performance developed? Accountability metrics are less likely to be effective when they are imposed from above, using standardized formulas developed by those far from active engagement with the activity being measured. Measurements are more likely to be meaningful when they are developed from the bottom up, with input from teachers, nurses, and the cop on the beat. That means asking those with the tacit knowledge that comes from direct experience to provide suggestions about how to develop appropriate performance standards.[2] Try to involve a representative group of those who will have a stake in the outcomes.[3] In the best of cases, they should continue to be part of the process of evaluating the measured data.

Remember that a system of measured performance will work to the extent that the people being measured believe in its worth. So far, in this chapter, we've taken the perspective of those in a position to decide whether and how to institute metrics. But what if you are not in such a position, if you're further down in the organizational hierarchy, where you are expected to execute metrics—a mid-level manager, say, or the head of an academic department? Then, you face a choice. If you believe in the goals for which the information is being collected, then your challenge is to provide accurate data in the most efficient way possible, one that demands the least time of you and those you manage. If, by contrast, you believe that the goals are dubious and the process wasteful, you might try to convince your superiors of that (perhaps by giving them a copy of this book). If that fails, then your task is to provide data in a way that takes the least time, meets minimal standards of acceptability, and won't harm your unit.

If you're near the *top* of the organization, making decisions about metrics, reread the previous paragraph, keeping in mind the different ways in which those below you might react. Metrics works best when those measured buy into its purposes and validity.[4]

9. Remember that *even the best measures are subject to corruption or goal diversion*. Insofar as individuals are agents out to maximize their own interests, there are inevitable drawbacks to all schemes of measured reward. If, as is currently still the case, doctors are remunerated based on the procedures they perform, that creates an incentive for them to perform too many procedures that have high costs but produce low benefits. But pay doctors based on the number of patients they see, and they have an incentive to see as many patients as possible, and to skimp on procedures that are time-consuming but potentially useful. Compensate them based on successful patient outcomes, and they are more likely to cream, avoiding the most problematic patients.[5]

That doesn't mean that performance measures should be abandoned just because they have some negative outcomes. Such metrics may still be worth using, despite their anticipatable problems: it's a matter of trade-offs. And that too is a matter of judgment.

10. Remember that sometimes, recognizing the limits of the possible is the beginning of wisdom. Not all problems are soluble, and even fewer are soluble by metrics. It's not true

that everything can be improved by measurement, or that everything that can be measured can be improved. Nor is making a problem more transparent necessarily a step to its solution. Transparency may make a troubling situation more salient, without making it more soluble.

In the end, there is no silver bullet, no substitute for actually knowing one's subject and one's organization, which is partly a matter of experience and partly a matter of unquantifiable skill. Many matters of importance are too subject to judgment and interpretation to be solved by standardized metrics. Ultimately, the issue is not one of metrics versus judgment, but metrics as informing judgment, which includes knowing how much weight to give to metrics, recognizing their characteristic distortions, and appreciating what can't be measured. In recent decades, too many politicians, business leaders, policymakers, and academic officials have lost sight of that.

ACKNOWLEDGMENTS

This book arose out of experiences recounted in the Introduction. I first formulated my thoughts in an article entitled, "The Costs of Accountability," which appeared in *The American Interest* (September–October 2015). I am grateful to Adam Garfinkle, the magazine's editor, for the alacrity with which he accepted the piece and the skill with which he edited it, and for permission to draw upon it for this book.

For encouragement and advice as the project grew from article to book I thank Eliot A. Cohen, Raphael Cohen, Harold James, Nathan Levitan, Elyse Parker, Thomas Patteson, Aviel Tucker, and Adrian Wooldridge. Joel Brenner and Arnold Kling were kind enough to read the manuscript and make useful suggestions for improvement, as did the late Christopher Kobrak. So too did my learned but worldly Catholic University colleagues, Caroline Sherman and Stephen West. I'm grateful to them all and to the many friends and colleagues who suggested sources and lines of inquiry. Four anonymous reviewers for Princeton University Press, moved purely by intrinsic motivation, gave generously of their time and helped me to refine my arguments.

Portions of the book were presented at seminars hosted by Rajshree Agarwal and David Sicilia at the Smith School of Business of the University of Maryland, College Park; by Daniel Klein at George Mason University's Department of Economics; and by Katherine Jansen at the Faculty Colloquium of the Department of History at the Catholic University of America. I've benefited from the feedback on each of those occasions.

For some years I have profited from an in-house, informal but ongoing seminar on organizational behavior, a seminar comprising my wife, our three children, and three children-in-law. They have shared their insights into the functions and dysfunctions of the organizational settings in which they have worked, which include government, education, and medicine. I am indebted to all of them, though none are responsible for the uses to which I have put their observations. Eli Muller first drew my attention to the larger themes of *The Wire* (episodes of which he can quote chapter and verse), and his acute analysis of institutional dynamics finds its echoes in the pages of this book, which he also helped to edit. Thanks go to Joseph Muller, M.D., for orienting me in the literature of medicine and healthcare, as well as his sage advice about the tone and direction of the book. My wife, Sharon, was the first reader and editor of every chapter, and many of the book's ideas were born or refined in our daily conversations (when we weren't talking about the immeasurable pleasures of grandparenthood—but that's the subject of another book).

Completion of this book was eased by the support of my parents. I am saddened to note that this is the last project that I was able to discuss with my father, Henry Muller, who passed away when the manuscript was nearing completion: his memory is a blessing. My mother, Bella Muller, remains a vigorous source of wisdom, encouragement, and humor in my life.

I am grateful to Jessica Yao of Princeton University Press for shepherding the project from manuscript to book, and to Linda Truilo for her copyediting of the manuscript.

For the past quarter century, Peter J. Dougherty has been not only my editor but an intellectual companion, feeding me a constant stream of books and ideas, and encouraging my efforts to write for audiences within and beyond the academy. He convinced me to develop the ideas first expressed in my article into this book, which he helped to shape at every stage of its development. To him the book is dedicated, with gratitude and abiding affection.

NOTES

INTRODUCTION

1. Gwyn Bevan and Christopher Hood, "What's Measured Is What Matters: Targets and Gaming in the English Public Health System," *Public Administration* 84, no. 3 (2006), pp. 517–53.

2. Paula Chatterjee and Karen E. Joynt, "Do Cardiology Quality Measures Actually Improve Patient Outcomes?" *Journal of the American Heart Association* (February 2014). The same problem was noted some years earlier by Richard Rothstein, "The Influence of Scholarship and Experience in Other Fields on Teacher Compensation Reform," pp. 87–110 in Matthew G. Springer (ed.), *Performance Incentives: Their Growing Impact on American K-12 Education* (Washington, D.C., 2009), p. 96; an expanded version was published as *Holding Accountability to Account: How Scholarship and Experience in Other Fields Inform Exploration of Performance Incentives in Education*, National Center on Performance Incentives, Working Paper 2008–04, February 2008.

3. Bevan and Hood, "What's Measured Is What Matters."

4. An exception is Richard Rothstein, *Holding Accountability to Account*. Also valuable is Adrian Perry, "Performance Indicators: 'Measure for Measure' or 'A Comedy of Errors'?" in Caroline Mager, Peter Robinson, et al. (eds.), *The New Learning Market* (London, 2000).

5. Laura Landro, "The Secret to Fighting Infections: Dr. Peter Pronovost Says It Isn't That Hard. If Only Hospitals Would Do It," *Wall Street Journal*, March 28, 2011, and Atul Gawande, *The Checklist Manifesto* (New York, 2009).

6. Michael Lewis, *Moneyball: The Art of Winning an Unfair Game* (New York, 2003).

7. Chris Lorenz, "If You're So Smart, Why Are You under Surveillance? Universities, Neoliberalism, and New Public Management," *Critical Inquiry* (Spring 2012), pp. 599–29, esp. pp. 610–11.

8. Jonathan Haidt, *The Righteous Mind* (New York, 2012), p. 34 and passim.

9. On the Spellings Commission report, see Fredrik deBoer, *Standardized Assessments of College Learning Past and Future* (Washington, D.C.: New American Foundation, March 2016).

10. Jerry Z. Muller, *The Mind and the Market: Capitalism in Modern European Thought* (New York, 2002) and my Teaching Company lecture course, "Thinking about Capitalism." See also Robert K. Merton, "The Unanticipated Consequences of Purposive Social Action," *American Sociological Review* 1 (December 1936), pp. 894–904; and Merton, "Unantici-

pated Consequences and Kindred Sociological Ideas: A Personal Gloss,"
in Carlo Mongardini and Simonetta Tabboni (eds.), *Robert K. Merton
and Contemporary Sociology* (New Brunswick, N.J., 1998), pp. 295–318;
Robert K. Merton and Elinor Barber, *The Travels and Adventures of Serendipity* (Princeton, 2004).

11. As Alfie Kohn notes, "[J]ust as social psychologists were starting to
recognize how counterproductive extrinsic motivators can be, this message was disappearing from publications in the field of management."
Kohn, *Punished by Rewards* (New York, 1999), p. 121.

CHAPTER 1. THE ARGUMENT IN A NUTSHELL

1. A term used by Bruce G. Charlton, "Audit, Accountability, Quality and
All That: The Growth of Managerial Technologies in UK Universities,"
in Stephen Prickett and Patricia Erskine-Hill (ed.), *Eduation! Education!
Education! Managerial Ethics and the Law of Unintended Consequences*
(Thorverton, England, 2002).

2. Fabrizio Ferraro, Jeffrey Pfeffer, and Robert L. Sutton, "Economics Language and Assumptions: How Theories Can Become Self-Fulfilling,"
Academy of Management Review 30, no. 1 (2005), pp. 8–24.

3. Tom Peters, "What Gets Measured Gets Done," (1986), http://tompeters
.com/columns/what-gets-measured-gets-done/.

4. I owe the latter formulation to Professor Paul Collier.

5. Charlton, "Audit, Accountability, Quality and All That," pp. 18–22.

6. Useful attempts to summarize these negative consequences include
Colin Talbot, "Performance Management," pp. 491–517 in Ewan Ferlie,
Laurence E. Lynn, Jr., and Christopher Pollitt (eds.), *The Oxford Hand-
book of Public Management* (New York, 2005), pp. 502–4; and Michael
Power, "The Theory of the Audit Explosion," pp. 326–44, in the same
volume, see esp. p. 335.

7. William Bruce Cameron, *Informal Sociology: A Casual Introduction to
Sociological Thinking* (New York, 1963).

8. Bevan and Hood, "What's Measured Is What Matters."

9. Quoted in Diane Ravitch, *The Death and Life of the Great American School
System* (New York, 2010), p. 160. See also Chris Shore, "Audit Culture
and Illiberal Governance: Universities and the Culture of Accountability," *Anthropological Theory* 8, no. 3 (2008), pp. 278–99; Mary Strathern
(ed.), *Audit Cultures: Anthropological Studies in Accountability, Ethics and
the Academy* (London, 2000).

10. Alison Wolf, *Does Education Matter? Myths about Education and Economic Growth* (London, 2002), p. 246. C.A.E. Goodhart, "Problems of Monetary Management: The UK Experience" (1975), pp. 91–121 in Goodhart, *Monetary Theory and Practice* (London, 1984).

CHAPTER 2. RECURRING FLAWS

1. Kurt C. Strange and Robert L. Ferrer, "The Paradox of Family Care," *Annals of Family Medicine* 7, no. 4 (July/August 2009), pp. 293–99, esp. p. 295.
2. Sally Engle Merry, *The Seductions of Quantification: Measuring Human Rights, Gender Violence, and Sex Trafficking* (Chicago, 2016), pp. 1–33.
3. Ibid., p. 1.
4. Kevin E. Davis, Benedict Kingsbury, and Sally Engle Merry, "Introduction: Global Governance by Indicators," in Kevin Davis, Angelina Fisher, Benedict Kingsbury, and Sally Engle Merry (eds.), *Governance by Indicators: Global Power through Quantification and Rankings* (New York, 2012), pp. 9, 18.

CHAPTER 3. THE ORIGINS OF MEASURING AND PAYING FOR PERFORMANCE

1. Quoted in Matthew Arnold, "The Twice-Revised Code" (1862), in R. H. Super (ed.), *The Complete Prose Works of Matthew Arnold* (Ann Arbor, Mich., 1960–77), vol. 2, pp. 214–15.
2. Park Honan, *Matthew Arnold: A Life* (Cambridge, Mass., 1983), pp. 318–19; R. H. Super's notes to Arnold, "The Twice-Revised Code," in *Complete Prose Works*, vol. 2, p. 349.
3. Arnold, "The Twice-Revised Code," pp. 223–24.
4. Ibid., p. 226.
5. Ibid., p. 243.
6. Fred G. Walcott, *The Origins of Culture and Anarchy: Matthew Arnold and Popular Education in England* (Toronto, 1970), pp. 7–8.
7. Arnold, "Special Report on Certain Points Connected with Elementary Education in Germany, Switzerland, and France" (1886), in *Complete Prose Works*, vol. 11, pp. 1, 28.
8. Simon Patten, "An Economic Measure of School Efficiency," *Educational Review* 41 (May 1911), pp. 467–69, quoted in Raymond E. Callahan, *Education and the Cult of Efficiency* (Chicago, 1962), p. 48.
9. Frederick W. Taylor, *The Principles of Scientific Management* (New York,

1911). On Taylor and his influence on education reform advocates see Callahan, *Education and the Cult of Efficiency*, chap. 2.

10. Alfred D. Chandler, Jr., *The Visible Hand: The Managerial Revolution in American Business* (Cambridge, Mass., 1977), pp. 275–76.

11. Taylor, quoted in James C. Scott, *Seeing Like a State: How Certain Schemes to Improve the Human Condition Have Failed* (New Haven, 1998), p. 336.

12. Frederick W. Taylor, *Principles of Scientific Management*, cited by David Montgomery, *The Fall of the House of Labor* (New Haven, 1989), p. 229.

13. Ellwood P. Cubberley, *Public School Administration* (Boston, 1916), on which see Callahan, *Education and the Cult of Efficiency*, pp. 95–99.

14. Dana Goldstein, *The Teacher Wars: A History of America's Most Embattled Profession* (New York, 2014), pp. 86–87.

15. For the term "student growth," see Chad Aldeman, "The Teacher Evaluation Revamp, in Hindsight," *EducationNext* 17, no. 2 (Spring 2017), http://educationnext.org/the-teacher-evaluation-revamp-in-hindsight-obama-administration-reform/.

16. Richard Sennett, *The Corrosion of Character: The Personal Consequences of Work in the New Capitalism* (New York, 1998), p. 42.

17. Rakesh Khurana, *From Higher Aims to Hired Hands: The Social Transformation of American Business Schools and the Unfulfilled Promise of Management as a Profession* (Princeton, 2007), p. 295.

18. Richard R. Locke and J.-C. Spender, *Confronting Managerialism: How the Business Elite and Their Schools Threw Our Lives out of Balance* (London, 2011), p. xiii.

19. Adrian Wooldridge, *Masters of Management* (New York, 2011), p. 3.

20. Bob Lutz, *Car Guys vs. Bean Counters: The Battle for the Soul of American Business* (New York, 2013).

21. Christopher Pollitt, "Towards a New World: Some Inconvenient Truths for Anglosphere Public Administration," *International Review of Administrative Sciences* 81, no. 1 (2015), pp. 3–17, esp. pp. 4–5; John Quiggin, "Bad Company: Correspondence," *Quarterlyessay.com*, https://www.quarterlyessay.com.au/correspondence/1203; similarly Henry Mintzberg, "Managing Government, Governing Management," *Harvard Business Review*, May–June 1996, pp. 75–83.

22. David Halberstam, *The Best and the Brightest* (New York, 1972), pp. 213–65.

23. Kenneth Cukier and Viktor Mayer-Schönberger, "The Dictatorship of Data," *MIT Technology Review*, May 31, 2013.

24. Edward N. Luttwak, *The Pentagon and the Art of War* (New York, 1984), p. 269.
25. Luttwak, *The Pentagon and the Art of War*, pp. 30–31. On the misuse of the metric of body counts, see the memoirs and scholarly literature analyzed in Ben Connable, *Embracing the Fog of War: Assessment and Metrics in Counterinsurgency* (Rand Corporation, 2012), pp. 106ff.
26. Luttwak, *The Pentagon and the Art of War*, pp. 138–43.
27. Ibid., p. 152.
28. Matthew Stewart, *The Management Myth: Why the Experts Keep Getting It Wrong* (New York, 2009), p. 31.
29. Theodore M. Porter, *Trust in Numbers: The Pursuit of Objectivity in Science and Public Life* (Princeton, 1995), p. ix.

CHAPTER 4. WHY METRICS BECAME SO POPULAR

1. Ralf Dahrendorf, *The Modern Social Conflict: An Essay on the Politics of Liberty* (Berkeley, 1988), p. 53.
2. Porter, *Trust in Numbers*, p. ix.
3. Stefan Collini, "Against Prodspeak," in Collini, *English Pasts: Essays in History and Culture* (Oxford, 1999), p. 239.
4. Philip K. Howard, *The Rule of Nobody: Saving America from Dead Laws and Broken Government* (New York, 2014), p. 44.
5. Philip K. Howard, *The Death of Common Sense: How Law Is Suffocating America* (New York, 1994), pp. 12, 27.
6. Howard, *The Rule of Nobody*, p. 54.
7. Lawrence M. Freedman, "The Litigation Revolution," in Michael Grossman and Christopher Tomlins (eds.), *The Cambridge History of Law in America: Vol. III The Twentieth Century and After* (Cambridge, 2008), p. 176.
8. Ibid., p. 187.
9. Ibid., p. 188–89.
10. Mark Schlesinger, "On Values and Democratic Policy Making: The Deceptively Fragile Consensus around Market-Oriented Medical Care," *Journal of Health Politics, Policy and Law* 27, no. 6 (December 2002), pp. 889–925; and Mark Schlesinger, "Choice Cuts: Parsing Policymakers' Pursuit of Patient Empowerment from an Individual Perspective," *Health, Economics, Policy and the Law* 5 (2010), pp. 365–87.
11. James Heilbrun, "Baumol's Cost Disease," in Ruth Towse (ed.), *A Handbook of Cultural Economics*, 2nd ed. (Cheltenham, England, 2011); and

William G. Bowen, "Costs and Productivity in Higher Education," The Tanner Lectures, Stanford University, October 2012, pp. 3–4.

12. Bowen, "Costs and Productivity in Higher Education," p. 5, citing Teresa A. Sullivan et al. (eds.), *Improving Measurement of Productivity in Higher Education* (Washington, D.C., 2012).

13. Yves Morieux and Peter Tollman, *Six Simple Rules: How to Manage Complexity Without Getting Complicated* (Boston, 2014), p. 6.

14. Rakesh Khurana, *Searching for a Corporate Savior: The Irrational Quest for Charismatic CEOs* (Princeton, 2002), esp. chap. 3. The phenomenon is by no means confined to the corporate sector.

15. Steven Levy, "A Spreadsheet Way of Knowledge," *Harper's*, November 1984, now online at https://medium.com/backchannel/a-spreadsheet -way-of-knowledge-8de60af7146e.

16. Seth Klarman, *A Margin of Safety: Risk-Averse Value Investing for the Thoughtful Investor* (New York, 1991).

CHAPTER 5. PRINCIPALS, AGENTS, AND MOTIVATION

1. Michael Jensen and William H. Meckling, "Theory of the Firm: Managerial Behavior, Agency Costs and Ownership Structure," *Journal of Financial Economics* 3, no. 4 (1976), pp. 305–60; Bengt Holmström and Paul Milgrom, "Multitask Principal-Agent Analyses: Incentive Contracts, Asset Ownership, and Job Design," *Journal of Law, Economics, & Organization* [Special Issue: Papers from the Conference on the New Science of Organization, January 1991] 7 (1991), pp. 24–52; Charles Wheelan, *Naked Economics,* rev. ed. (New York, 2010), pp. 39–43.

2. Khurana, *From Higher Aims to Hired Hands*, pp. 317–26. Similarly, Richard Münch, *Globale Eliten, lokale Autoritäten* (Frankfurt, 2009), p. 75. Also instructive is Ferraro, Pfeffer, Sutton, "Economics Language and Assumptions."

3. Theodore M. Porter, *Trust in Numbers: The Pursuit of Objectivity in Science and Public Life* (Princeton, 1995), p. ix.

4. Talbot, "Performance Management," p. 497.

5. David Chinitz and Victor G. Rodwin, "What Passes and Fails as Health Policy and Management," *Journal of Health Politics, Policy, and Law* 39, no. 5 (October 2014), pp. 1113–26, esp. pp. 1114–17.

6. Mintzberg, "Managing Government, Governing Management," pp. 75–83; and Holmström and Milgrom, "Multitask Principal-Agent Analyses."

7. Hal K. Rainey and Young Han Chun, "Public and Private Management

Compared," in Ewan Ferlie, Laurence E. Lynn, Jr., and Christopher Pollitt (eds.), *The Oxford Handbook of Public Management* (New York, 2005), pp. 72–102, 85; and James Q. Wilson, *Bureaucracy: What Government Agencies Do and Why They Do It* (New York, 2000), pp. 156–57.

8. Roland Bénabout and Jean Tirole, "Intrinsic and Extrinsic Motivation," *Review of Economic Studies* no. 70 (2003), pp. 489–520. A pioneering work of intrinsic motivation theory was Edward L. Deci, *Intrinsic Motivation* (New York, 1975). Other studies by psychologists include Thane S. Pittman, Jolee Emery, and Ann K. Boggiano, "Intrinsic and Extrinsic Motivational Orientations: Reward-Induced Changes in Preference for Complexity," *Journal of Personality and Social Psychology* 42, no. 5 (1982), pp. 789–97; and T. S. Pittman, A. K. Boggiano, and D. N. Ruble, "Intrinsic and Extrinsic Motivational Orientations: Limiting Conditions on the Undermining and Enhancing Effects of Reward on Intrinsic Motivation," in J. Levine and M. Wang (eds.), *Teacher and Student Perceptions: Implications for Learning* (Hillsdale, N.J., 1983). An important figure in the transition of the theory from psychology to economics is Bruno S. Frey, whose works include *Not Just for the Money: An Economic Theory of Human Motivation* (Cheltenham, England, 1997). For a review of the relevant literature with a focus on behavioral economics, which concludes that "behavioral economics clearly shows that the universal application of pay-for-performance as practiced today is not warranted by scientific facts," see Antoinette Weibel, Meike Wiemann, and Margit Osterloh, "A Behavioral Economics Perspective on the Overjustification Effect: Crowding-In and Crowding-Out of Intrinsic Motivation," in Marylène Gagné (ed.), *The Oxford Handbook of Work Engagement, Motivation, and Self-Determination Theory* (New York, 2014).

9. Pittman, Boggiano, and Ruble, "Intrinsic and Extrinsic Motivational Orientations."

10. Bénabout and Tirole, "Intrinsic and Extrinsic Motivation," p. 504.

11. Bruno S. Frey and Margit Osterloh, "Motivate People with Prizes," *Nature* 465, no. 17 (June 2010), p. 871.

12. George Akerlof, "Labor Contracts as a Partial Gift Exchange," *Quarterly Journal of Economics* 97, no. 4 (1982), 543–69.

13. Bruno S. Frey and Reto Jegen, "Motivation Crowding Theory," *Journal of Economic Surveys* 15, no. 5 (2001), pp. 589–611; and Robert Gibbons, "Incentives in Organizations," *Journal of Economic Perspectives* 12, no. 4 (Fall 1998), pp. 115–32, esp. p. 129.

14. Gibbons, "Incentives in Organizations."

15. Talbot, "Performance Management," pp. 491–517; Adrian Wooldridge, *Masters of Management* (New York, 2011), pp. 318–19; Pollitt, "Towards a New World"; Christopher Hood, "The 'New Public Management in the 1980s: Variations on a Theme," *Accounting, Organization, and Society* 20, nos. 2/3 (1995), pp. 93–109; Christopher Hood and Guy Peters, "The Middle Aging of New Public Management: Into the Age of Paradox?" *Journal of Public Administration Research and Theory* 14, no. 3 (2004), pp. 267–82. On the background and early history of NPM in the United Kingdom and the United States, see Christopher Pollitt, *Managerialism and the Public Services,* 2nd ed. (Oxford, 1993).

CHAPTER 6. PHILOSOPHICAL CRITIQUES

1. Harry Braverman, *Labor and Monopoly Capital* (New York, 1974).
2. Michael Oakeshott, "Rationalism in Politics" (1947) in Oakeshott, *Rationalism in Politics and Other Essays* (Indianapolis, 1991).
3. Friedrich Hayek, "The Uses of Knowledge in Society," "The Meaning of Competition," and "'Free' Enterprise and Competitive Order," all in Hayek, *Individualism and Economic Order* (Chicago, 1948).
4. Wolf, *Does Education Matter?* p. 246; Lorenz, "If You're So Smart"; Bevan and Hood, "What's Measured Is What Matters." For an extended analysis of the ways in which the British higher education regime replicates features of the Soviet system, see Aviezer Tucker, "Bully U: Central Planning and Higher Education," *Independent Review* 17, no. 1 (Summer 2012), pp. 99–119.
5. Alfie Kohn, *Punished by Rewards* (New York, 1999), pp. 62ff; and Teresa Amabile, "How to Kill Creativity," *Harvard Business Review* (September–October 1998).
6. Scott, *Seeing Like a State,* p. 313.
7. Isaiah Berlin, "Political Judgment," in Berlin, *The Sense of Reality: Studies in Ideas and Their History,* ed. Henry Hardy (New York, 1996), pp. 53, 50.
8. Elie Kedourie *Diamonds into Glass: The Government and the Universities* (London, 1988), reprinted in Elie Kedourie, "The British Universities under Duress," *Minerva* 31, no. 1 (March, 1993), pp. 56–105.
9. Elie Kedourie, *Perekstroika in the Universities* (London, 1989), pp. x–xi.
10. Kedourie, *Perestroika,* p. 29.
11. Kedourie "The British Universities under Duress," p. 61.
12. Background information on GPRA at http://www.foreffectivegov.org/node/326, and Donald P. Moynihan and Stephane Lavertu, "Does Involvement in Performance Management Routines Encourage Perfor-

mance Information Use? Evaluating GPRA and PART" *Public Administration Review* 72, no. 4 (July/August 2012), pp. 592–602.

CHAPTER 7. COLLEGES AND UNIVERSITIES

1. Department of Education, "For Public Feedback: A College Ratings Framework" (December, 2014), http://www2.ed.gov/documents/college -affordability/college-ratings-fact-sheet.pdf.
2. https://www.luminafoundation.org/files/publications/stronger _nation/2016/A_Stronger_Nation-2016-National.pdf.
3. Wolf, *Does Education Matter?*
4. Wolf, *Does Education Matter?*; Jaison R. Abel, Richard Deitz, and Yaquin Su, "Are Recent College Graduates Finding Good Jobs?" *Federal Reserve Bank of New York: Current Issues in Economics and Finance* 20, no. 1 (2014); Paul Beaudry, David A. Green, Benjamin M. Sand, "The Great Reversal in the Demand for Skill and Cognitive Tasks," NBER Working Paper 18901, March 2013.
5. See, for example, Katherine Mangan, "High-School Diploma Options Multiply, but May Not Set Up Students for College Success," *Chronicle of Higher Education*, October 19, 2015.
6. Scott Jaschik, "ACT Scores Drop as More Take Test," *Inside Higher Education*, August 24, 2016; and "ACT Scores Down for 2016 U.S. Grad Class Due to Increased Percentage of Students Tested," http://www.act.org /content/act/en/newsroom/act-scores-down-for-2016-us-grad-class-due -to-increased-percentage-of-students-tested.html.
7. William G. Bowen and Michael S. McPherson, *Lesson Plan: An Agenda for Change in American Higher Education* (Princeton, 2016), p. 30.
8. See, for example, Tucker, "Bully U," p. 104.
9. Valen E. Johnson, *Grade Inflation: A Crisis in College Education* (New York, 2003).
10. John Bound, Michael F. Lovenheim, and Sarah Turner, "Increasing Time to Baccalaureate Degree in the United States," NBER Working Paper 15892, April 2010, p. 13; and Sarah E. Turner, "Going to College and Finishing College. Explaining Different Educational Outcomes," in Caroline M. Hoxby (ed.) *College Choices: The Economics of Where to Go, When to Go, and How to Pay for It* (Chicago, 2004), pp. 13–62, http://www .nber.org/chapters/c10097, passim.
11. Arnold Kling and John Merrifield, "Goldin and Katz and Education Policy Failings," *Econ Journal Watch* 6, no. 1 (January 2009), pp. 2–20, esp. p. 14.

12. Wolf, *Does Education Matter?* chap. 7.
13. Lorelle L. Espinosa, Jennifer R. Crandall, and Malika Tukibayeva, *Rankings, Institutional Behavior, and College and University Choice* (Washington, D.C., American Council on Education, 2014), p. 12.
14. Wolf, *Does Education Matter?* chap. 7; similarly Daron Acemoglu and David Autor, "What Does Human Capital Do?" *Journal of Economic Literature* 50, no. 2 (2012), pp. 426–63.
15. Wolf, *Does Education Matter?* chaps. 2 and 6; Paul Beaudry, David A. Green, and Benjamin M. Sand, "The Great Reversal in the Demand for Skill and Cognitive Tasks," NBER Working Paper 18901, March 2013.
16. Stuart Eizenstat and Robert Lerman, "Apprenticeships Could Help U.S. Workers Gain a Competitive Edge" (Washington, D.C., Urban Institute, May 2013); Mark P. Mills, "Are Skilled Trades Doomed to Decline?" Manhattan Institute, New York, 2016, http://www.manhattan-institute.org/sites/default/files/IB-MM-1016.pdf.
17. Thomas Hale and Gonzalo Viña, "University Challenge: The Race for Money, Students and Status," *Financial Times*, June 23, 2016; https://www.oecd.org/unitedkingdom/United%20Kingdom-EAG2014-Country-Note.pdf. Stefan Collini, in *What Are Universities For?* gives a figure of 45 percent in 2012 for enrollment in higher education.
18. For a brief history, see Stefan Collini, *What Are Universities For?* chap. 2.
19. Wolf, *Does Education Matter?* chap. 7.
20. Shore, "Audit Culture and Illiberal Governance," pp. 289–90. See also James Wilsdon et al., *The Metric Tide: Report of the Independent Review of the Role of Metrics in Research Assessment and Management* (July 2015).
21. Stephen Prickett, Introduction to *Education! Education! Education!*
22. Charlton, "Audit, Accountability, Quality and All That," p. 23.
23. http://www2.ed.gov/admins/finaid/accred/accreditation_pg6.html.
24. Peter Augustine Lawler, "Truly Higher Education," *National Affairs* (Spring 2015), pp. 114–30, esp. pp. 120–21.
25. Charlton, "Audit, Accountability, Quality and All That," p. 22; and Lorenz, "If You're So Smart," p. 609.
26. Benjamin Ginsberg, *The Fall of the Faculty: The Rise of the All Administrative University* (Baltimore, 2013).
27. Craig Totterow and James Evans, "Reconciling the Small Effect of Rankings on University Performance with the Transformational Cost of Conformity" in Elizabeth Popp Berman and Catherine Paradeise (eds.), *The University under Pressure*, Research in the Sociology of Or-

ganizations, vol. 4 (Bingley, England, 2016), pp. 265–301, and Tucker, "Bully U," p. 114.

28. Wendy Nelson Espeland and Michael Sauder, "Rankings and Reactivity: How Public Measures Re-create Social Worlds," *American Journal of Sociology* 113, no. 1 (July 2007), pp. 1–40, esp. p. 11.

29. Ibid., p. 25.

30. Ibid., p. 26.

31. Ibid., pp. 30–31. For more on how some law schools game the statistics, see Alex Wellen, "The $8.78 Million Maneuver," *New York Times,* July 31, 2005. For more on how universities attempt to rise in the rankings, see Wendy Nelson Espeland and Michael Sauder, "The Dynamism of Indicators" in Davis et al. (eds.) *Governance by Indicators*, pp. 103–5.

32. See, for example, Doug Lederman, "'Manipulating,' Er, Influencing 'U.S. News,'" *Inside Higher Ed*, June 3, 2009.

33. Totterow and Evans, "Reconciling the Small Effect of Rankings on University Performance with the Transformatonal Cost of Conformity."

34. On the early history of this, see Collini, *What Are Universities For?* chap. 6, "Bibliometry."

35. Prickett, Introduction to *Education! Education! Education!* p. 7.

36. Peter Weingart, "Impact of Bibliometrics upon the Science System: Inadvertent Consequences," *Scientometrics* 62, no. 1 (2005), pp. 117–31, esp. p. 126.

37. Ibid., p. 127; see also Christian Fleck, "Impact Factor Fetishism," *European Journal of Sociology* 54, no. 2 (2013), pp. 327–56. On the difficulties of comparing research productivity among disciplines, see Dorothea Jansen et al., "Drittmittel als Performanzindikator der wissenschaftlichen Forschung: Zum Einfluss von Rahmenbedingungen auf Forschungsleistung," *Kölner Zeitschrift für Soziologie und Sozialpsychologie* 59, no 1 (2007), pp. 125–49.

38. See on these issues, Weingart, "Impact of Bibliometrics upon the Science System," and Michael Power, "Research Evaluation in the Audit Society," in Hildegard Matthies and Dagmar Simon (eds.), *Wissenschaft unter Beobachtung: Effekte und Defekte von Evaluationen* (Wiesbaden, 2008), pp. 15–24.

39. Carl T. Bergstrom, "Use Ranking to Help Search," *Nature* 465, no. 17 (June 2010), p. 870.

40. Espeland and Sauder, "Rankings and Reactivity," p. 15. See too Münch, *Globale Eliten, lokale Autoritäten.*

41. Espinosa, Crandall, and Tukibayeva, *Rankings, Institutional Behavior, and College and University Choice*; Douglas Belkin, "Obama Spells Out College-Ranking Framework," *Wall Street Journal*, December 19, 2014; Jack Stripling, "Obama's Legacy: An Unlikely Hawk on Higher Ed," *Chronicle of Higher Education*, September 30, 2016.

42. Jonathan Rothwell, "Understanding the College Scorecard," paper, Brookings Institution, September 28, 2015, https://www.brookings.edu /opinions/understanding-the-college-scorecard/; Beckie Supiano, "Early Evidence Shows College Scorecard Matters, but Only to Some," *Chronicle of Higher Education*, May 27, 2016.

43. See Lauren A. Rivera, *Pedigree: How Elite Students Get Elite Jobs* (Princeton, 2015); and Elizabeth A. Armstrong and Laura T. Hamilton, *Paying for the Party: How College Maintains Inequality* (Cambridge, Mass., 2013).

44. Rothwell, "Understanding the College Scorecard."

45. Jeffrey Steedle, "On the Foundations of Standardized Assessment of College Outcomes and Estimating Value Added," in K. Carey and M. Schneider (eds.), *Accountability in Higher Education* (New York, 2010), p. 8.

46. See, among many other critiques, Nicholas Tampio, "College Ratings and the Idea of the Liberal Arts, *JSTOR Daily*, July 8, 2015, http://daily .jstor.org/college-ratings-idea-liberal-arts/, and James B. Stewart, "College Rankings Fail to Measure the Influence of the Institution," *New York Times*, October 2, 2015.

47. Robert Grant, "Education, Utility and the Universities" in Prickett and Erskine-Hill (eds.), *Education! Education! Education!* p. 52.

48. See Rivera, *Pedigree*, p. 78 and passim.

49. Espinosa, Crandall, and Tukibayeva, *Rankings, Institutional Behavior, and College and University Choice*, p. 9.

CHAPTER 8. SCHOOLS

1. Ravitch, *The Death and Life of the Great American School System*, p. 149.

2. T. S. Dee and B. Jacob, "The Impact of 'No Child Left Behind' on Student Achievement," *Journal of Policy Analysis and Management* 30 (2011), pp. 418–46.

3. Jesse Rhodes, *An Education in Politics: The Origins and Evolution of No Child Left Behind* (Ithaca, N.Y., 2012), p. 88.

4. Quoted in ibid., p. 88.

5. Ibid., p. 153.

6. Goldstein, *Teacher Wars*, p. 188.

7. Diane Ravitch, *Reign of Error* (New York, 2013), p. 51 and charts on pp. 340–42; and Kristin Blagg and Matthew M. Chingos, *Varsity Blues: Are High School Students Being Left Behind?* (Washington, D.C.: Urban Institute, May 2016), pp. 3–5.

8. Dee and Jacob, "The Impact of 'No Child Left Behind' on Student Achievement," pp. 418–46. See also, Ravitch, *The Death and Life of the Great American School System*, pp. 107–8, 159; Goldstein, *Teacher Wars*, p. 187; and American Statistical Association, "ASA Statement on Using Value-Added Models for Educational Assessment, April 8, 2014," https://www.amstat.org/policy/pdfs/ASA_VAM_Statement.pdf.

9. Goldstein, *Teacher Wars*, p. 226.

10. Ibid. For an argument in favor of value-added testing over evaluating schools based on "proficiency" or "college-readiness," see Michael J. Petrilli and Aaron Churchill, "Why States Should Use Student Growth, and Not Proficiency Rates, when Gauging School Effectiveness," Thomas Fordham Institute, October 13, 2016, https://edexcellence.net/articles/why-states-should-use-student-growth-and-not-proficiency-rates-when-gauging-school.

11. Martin R. West, written statement to U.S. Senate Committee on Health, Education, Labor, and Pensions, January 21, 2015, http://www.help.senate.gov/imo/media/doc/West.pdf, and David J. Deming et al., "When Does Accountability Work?" *educationnext.org* (Winter 2016), pp. 71–76. On Florida, David N. Figlio and Lawrence S. Getzler, "Accountability, Ability, and Disability: Gaming the System," NBER Working Paper No. 9307, October 2002.

12. On Houston and Dallas, see Ravitch, *Death and Life*, p. 155; on Atlanta, see Rachel Aviv, "Wrong Answer: In an Era of High-Stakes Testing, a Struggling School Made a Shocking Choice," *The New Yorker*, July 21, 2014, pp. 54–65; on Chicago, see Brian A. Jacob and Steven D. Levitt, "Rotten Apples: An Investigation of the Prevalence and Predictors of Teacher Cheating," *Quarterly Journal of Economics* 118, no. 3 (August, 2003), pp. 843–77; on "scrubbing" in Cleveland, Ravitch, *Death and Life*, p. 159. Also Goldstein, *Teacher Wars*, p. 227.

13. Goldstein, *Teacher Wars*, pp. 186, 209.

14. Alison Wolf, *Does Education Matter?* Similarly, Donald T. Campbell, "[A]chievement tests may well be valuable indicators of general school achievement under conditions of normal teaching aimed at general competence. But when test scores become the goal of the teaching

process, they both lose their value as indicators of educational status and distort the educational process in undesirable ways," quoted in Mark Palko and Andrew Gelman, "How Schools that Obsess about Standardized Tests Ruin Them as Measures of Success," *Vox: Policy and Politics*, August 16, 2016, http://www.vox.com/2016/8/16/12482748/success-academy-schools-standardized-tests-metrics-charter.

15. "We believe that the system is now out of balance in the sense that the drive to meet government-set targets has too often become the goal rather than the means to the end of providing the best possible education for all children. This is demonstrated in phenomena such as teaching to the test, narrowing the curriculum and focusing disproportionate resources on borderline pupils. We urge the Government to reconsider its approach in order to create incentives to schools to teach the whole curriculum and acknowledge children's achievements in the full range of the curriculum. The priority should be a system which gives teachers, parents and children accurate information about children's progress." (Paragraph 82). Select Committee on Children, Schools and Families, Third Report (2008). http://www.publications.parliament.uk/pa/cm200708/cmselect/cmchilsch/169/16912.htm.

16. Rhodes, *An Education in Politics*, p. 176.

17. Goldstein, *Teacher Wars*, pp. 213–17.

18. Goldstein, *Teacher Wars*, pp. 207–8.

19. Roland Fryer, "Teacher Incentives and Student Achievement: Evidence from New York City Public Schools," NBER Working Paper No. 16850, March 2011.

20. Goldstein, *Teacher Wars*, pp. 224–26.

21. See the studies cited in Kohn, *Punished by Rewards*, p. 334, fn. 37.

22. Fryer, "Teacher Incentives and Student Achievement," p. 3.

23. Frederick M. Hess, "Our Achievement-Gap Mania," *National Affairs* (Fall 2011), pp. 113–29.

24. Lauren Musu-Gillette et al., *Status and Trends in the Educational Achievement of Racial and Ethnic Groups 2016* (Washington, D.C.: National Center for Educational Statistics, 2016), p. iv.

25. For a recent confirmation of the Coleman Report's original findings, and of their ongoing relevance, see Stephen L. Morgan and Sol Bee Jung, "Still No Effect of Resources, Even in the New Gilded Age," *Russell Sage Foundation Journal of the Social Sciences* 2, no. 5 (2016), pp. 83–116.

26. Sean F. Reardon, *The Widening Achievement Gap between the Rich and*

the Poor: New Evidence and Some Possible Explanations (Russell Sage Foundation, 2012), downloaded from https://cepa.stanford.edu/content/widening-academic-achievement-gap-between-rich-and-poor-new-evidence-and-possible.

27. Edward C. Banfield, *The Unheavenly City Revisited* (New York, 1974), pp. 273–74.

28. Among economists, the significance of these qualities has been emphasized by James Heckman, "Schools, Skills, and Synapses," *Economic Inquiry* 46, no. 3 (July 2008), pp. 289–324. Of course, their importance has long been taken for granted by those not wedded to metric fixation. Character qualities of self-control and the ability to defer gratification, however, are themselves linked to cognitive ability, see Richard E. Nisbett et al., "Intelligence: New Findings and Theoretical Developments," *American Psychologist* 67, no. 2 (2012), pp. 130–59, esp. p. 151.

29. Alexandria Neason, "Welcome to Kindergarten. Take This Test. And This One." *Slate*, March 4, 2015.

30. Nisbett et al., "Intelligence," p. 138.

31. Angela Duckworth, "Don't Grade Schools on Grit," *New York Times*, March 27, 2016.

32. Hess, "Our Achievement-Gap Mania," and Wolf, *Does Education Matter?* The declining support for programs for gifted children in Europe is noted in Tom Clynes "How to Raise a Genius: Lessons from a 45-Year Study of Super-smart Children," *Nature* 537, no. 7619 (September 7, 2016).

33. Ravitch, *Death and Life*, passim., and Kenneth Berstein, "Warning from the Trenches: A High School Teacher Tells College Educators What They Can Expect in the Wake of 'No Child Left Behind' and 'Race to the Top,'" *Academe* (January–February 2013), http://www.aaup.org/article/warnings-trenches#.VN62JMZQ2AE; and the powerful testimony of "Teacher of the Year" Anthony J. Mullen, "Teachers Should be Seen and Not Heard," *Education Week*, January 7, 2010, http://blogs.edweek.org/teachers/teacher_of_the_year/2010/01/teachers_should_be_seen_and_no.html.

CHAPTER 9. MEDICINE

1. Sean P. Keehan et al., "National Health Expenditure Projections, 2015–2025: Economy, Prices, and Aging Expected to Shape Spending and Enrollment," *Health Affairs* 35, no. 8 (August 2016), pp. 1–10; Atul Gawande, "The Checklist," *New Yorker*, December 10, 2007.

2. *World Health Report 2000, Health Systems: Improving Performance*, quoted

in Scott Atlas, *In Excellent Health: Setting the Record Straight on America's Health Care* (Stanford, Calif., 2011).

3. Atlas, *In Excellent Health.*
4. Ibid., pp. 28–30, 99–105.
5. Ibid., p. 84; and David M. Cutler, Adriana Lleras-Muney, and Tom Vogl, "Socioeconomic Status and Health: Dimensions and Mechanisms," in Sherry Glied and Peter C. Smith (eds.), *The Oxford Handbook of Health Economics* (New York, 2011), pp. 124–63, esp. 147–53.
6. Atlas, *In Excellent Health*, p. 156.
7. Michael E. Porter and Thomas H. Lee, "The Strategy That Will Fix Health Care," *Harvard Business Review* (October 2013), pp. 50–70, esp. 56.
8. The discussion of Geisinger is based on Douglas McCarthy, Kimberly Mueller, and Jennifer Wrenn, *Geisinger Health System: Achieving the Potential of Integration through Innovation, Leadership, Measurement, and Incentives* (Commonweatlh Fund Case Study, June 2009), and Glenn D. Steele, Jr., "A Proven New Model for Reimbursing Physicians," *Harvard Business Review* (September 15, 2015), by the former CEO of Geisinger.
9. Peter J. Pronovost et al., "Sustaining Reductions in Central Line-Associated Bloodstream Infections in Michigan Intensive Care Units: A 10-Year Analysis," *American Journal of Medical Quality* 31, no. 3 (2016), pp. 197–202.
10. Chinitz and Rodwin, "What Passes and Fails as Health Policy and Management," p. 1117.
11. For example, Patrick Conway, Farzad Mostashari, and Carolyn Clancy, "The Future of Quality Measurement for Improvement and Accountability," *JAMA* [*Journal of the American Medical Association*] 309, no. 21 (June 5, 2013), pp. 2215–16; James F. Burgess and Andrew Street, "Measuring Organizational Performance," in Sherry Glied and Peter C. Smith (eds.), *The Oxford Handbook of Health Economics* (New York, 2011), pp. 688–706, esp. p. 701; David M. Shahian et al., "Rating the Raters: The Inconsistent Quality of Health Care Performance Measurement," *Annals of Surgery* 264, no. 1 (July 2016), pp. 36–38; J. Matthew Austin, Elizabeth A. McGlynn, and Peter J. Pronovost, "Fostering Transparency in Outcomes, Quality, Safety, and Costs," *JAMA* 316, no. 16 (October 25, 2016), pp. 1661–62.
12. On the propensity to call for better metrics, see Chinitz and Rodwin, "What Passes and Fails as Health Policy and Management," p. 1120.
13. Jason H. Wasfy et al., "Public Reporting in Cardiovascular Medicine:

Accountability, Unintended Consequences, and Promise for Improvement," *Circulation* 131, no. 17 (April 28, 2015), pp. 1518–27.

14. Chinitz and Rodwin, "What Passes and Fails as Health Policy and Management," p. 1118.

15. N. A. Ketallar et al., "Public Release of Performance Data in Changing the Behaviour of Healthcare Consumers, Professionals or Organisations" *Cochrane Database System Review*, Nov. 9, 2011.

16. Gary Y. Young, Howard Beckman, and Errol Baker, "Financial Incentives, Professional Values and Performance," *Journal of Organizational Behavior* 33 (2012), pp. 964–983.

17. Elaine M. Burns, Chris Pettengell, Thanos Athanasious, and Ara Darzi, "Understanding the Strengths and Weaknesses of Public Reporting of Surgeon-Specific Outcomes," *Health Affairs* 35, no. 3 (March 2016), pp. 415–21, esp. p. 416.

18. D. Blumenthal, E. Malphrus, and J. M. McGinnis (eds.), *Vital Signs: Core Metrics for Health and Health Care Progress* (Washington, 2015), p. 90. On the use of "star ratings" by the National Health Service in England, see Bevan and Hood "What's Measured Is What Matters."

19. Chinitz and Rodwin, "What Passes and Fails as Health Policy and Management," pp. 1114–19.

20. Karen E. Joynt et al., "Public Reporting of Mortality Rates for Hospitalized Medicare Patients and Trends in Mortality for Reported Conditions," *Annals of Internal Medicine,* published online May 31, 2016.

21. M. W. Friedberg et al., "A Methodological Critique of the ProPublica Surgeon Scorecard" (Rand Corporation, Santa Monica, Calif., 2015), http://www.rand.org/pubs/perspectives/PE170.html, and David M. Shahian et al., "Rating the Raters: The Inconsistent Quality of Health Care Performance Measurement," *Annals of Surgery* 264, no. 1 (July 2016), pp. 36–38.

22. Cheryl L. Damberg et al., *Measuring Success in Health Care Value-Based Purchasing Programs: Summary and Recommendations* (Rand Corporation, 2014), p. 18. Rachel M. Werner et al., "The Effect of Pay-for-Performance in Hospitals: Lessons for Quality Improvement," *Health Affairs* 30, no. 4 (April 2011), pp. 690–98. Similarly, and most recently, Aaron Mendelson et al., "The Effects of Pay-for-Performance Programs on Health, Health Care Use, and Processes of Care: A Systematic Review," *Annals of Internal Medicine* 165, no. 5 (March 7, 2017), pp. 341–53.

23. Patricia Ingraham, "Of Pigs in Pokes and Policy Diffusion: Another

Look at Pay for Performance," *Public Administration Review* 53 (1993), pp. 348–56; Christopher Hood and Guy Peters, "The Middle Aging of New Public Management: Into the Age of Paradox?" *Journal of Public Administration Research and Theory* 14, no. 3 (2004), pp. 267–82; Chinitz and Rodwin, "What Passes and Fails as Health Policy and Management," pp. 1113–26.

24. Martin Roland and Stephen Campbell, "Successes and Failures of Pay for Performance in the United Kingdom," *New England Journal of Medicine* 370 (May 15, 2014), pp. 1944–49. The phrase "treating to the test" comes from Chinitz and Rodwin, "What Passes and Fails as Health Policy and Management," p. 1115.

25. Burns et al., "Understanding the Strengths and Weaknesses of Public Reporting of Surgeon-Specific Outcomes," p. 418; and Wasfy et al., "Public Reporting in Cardiovascular Medicine"; and K. E. Joynt et al., "Association of Public Reporting for Percutaneous Coronary Intervention with Utilization and Outcomes among Medicare Beneficiaries with Acute Myocardial Infarction," *JAMA* 308, no. 14 (2012), pp. 1460–68; Joel M. Kupfer, "The Morality of Using Mortality as a Financial Incentive: Unintended Consequences and Implications for Acute Hospital Care," *JAMA* 309, no. 21 (June 3, 2013), pp. 2213–14.

26. Richard Lilford and Peter Pronovost, "Using Hospital Mortality Rates to Judge Hospital Performance: A Bad Idea that Just Won't Go Away," *British Medical Journal* (April 10, 2010).

27. Ibid.

28. D. Blumenthal, E. Malphrus, and J. M. McGinnis (eds.), *Vital Signs: Core Metrics for Health and Health Care Progress* (Washington, D.C., 2015).

29. Ibid., pp. 90–91.

30. Robert Pear, "Shaping Health Policy for Millions, and Still Treating Some on the Side," *New York Times*, March 29, 2016.

31. Donald M. Berwick, "The Toxicity of Pay for Performance," *Quality Management in Health Care* 4, no. 1 (1995), pp. 27–33.

32. Wasfy et al., "Public Reporting in Cardiovascular Medicine"; Claire Noel-Mill and Keith Lind, "Is Observation Status Substituting for Hospital Readmission?" *Health Affairs Blog*, October 28, 2015; as well as https://www.medicare.gov/hospitalcompare/Data/30-day-measures .html.

33. David Himmelstein and Steffie Woolhandler, "Quality Improvement: 'Become Good at Cheating and You Never Need to Become Good at Anything Else'" *Health Affairs Blog*, August 27, 2015.

34. Sabriya Rice, "Medicare Readmission Penalties Create Quality Metrics Stress," *Modern Healthcare*, August 8, 2015.
35. Shannon Muchmore, "Bill Targets Socio-economic Factors in Hospital Readmissions," *Modern Healthcare*, May 19, 2016.
36. See for example Michael L. Barnett, John Hsu, and Michael J. McWilliams, "Patient Characteristics and Differences in Hospital Readmission Rates," *JAMA Internal Medicine* 175, no. 11 (November 2015), pp. 1803–12; and Shannon Muchmore, "Readmissions May Say More about Patients than Care," *Modern Healthcare* (September 14, 2015).

CHAPTER 10. POLICING

1. Barry Latzer, *The Rise and Fall of Violent Crime in America* (San Francisco, 2016).
2. On Compstat, see Ken Peak and Emmanuel P. Barthe "Community Policing and CompStat: Merged, or Mutually Exclusive?" *The Police Chief* 76, no. 12 (December 2009); John Eterno and Eli Silverman, *The Crime Numbers Game: Management by Manipulation* (Boca Raton, 2012); Heather Mac Donald, "Compstat and Its Enemies," *City Journal*, February 17, 2010, offers a critique of earlier claims by Eterno and Silverman.
3. Donald T. Campbell, "Assessing the Impact of Planned Social Change" (1976), *Journal of Multidisciplinary Evaluation* (February 2011), p. 34.
4. See, for example, David Bernstein and Noah Isackson, "The Truth about Chicago's Crime Rates: Part 2," *Chicago Magazine*, May 19, 2014.
5. Mac Donald, "Compstat and Its Enemies."
6. "Police Fix Crime Statistics to Meet Targets, MPs Told," BBC News, November 19, 2013, http://www.bbc.com/news/uk-25002927.
7. Ed Burns interview on "Fresh Air," National Public Radio, November 22, 2006. See also David Simon interview with Bill Moyers, at www.pbs.org/moyers/journal/04172009/transcript1.html.
8. Campbell, "Assessing the Impact," p. 35.

CHAPTER 11. THE MILITARY

1. Jonathan Schroden, a scholar at the Naval War College, concludes that current methods of COIN assessment are so faulty that it would be better to "stop doing operations assessments altogether." Jonathan Schroden, "Why Operations Assessments Fail: It's Not Just the Metrics," *Naval War College Review* 64, no. 4 (Autumn 2011), pp. 89–102, esp. 99.
2. Connable, *Embracing the Fog of War*, chap. 6.

3. David Kilcullen, *Counterinsurgency* (New York, 2010), p. 2.
4. Ibid., pp. 56–57.
5. Ibid., pp. 58–59.
6. Ibid., p. 60.
7. Connable, *Embracing the Fog of War*, pp. xv, xx.
8. Jan Osborg et al., *Assessing Locally Focused Stability Operations* (Rand Corporation, 2014), p. 9.
9. Connable, *Embracing the Fog of War*, p. 29.

CHAPTER 12. BUSINESS AND FINANCE

1. http://www.simon.rochester.edu/fac/misra/mkt_salesforce.pdf.
2. Barry Gruenberg, "The Happy Worker: An Analysis of Educational and Occupational Differences in Determinants of Job Satisfaction," *American Journal of Sociology* 86 (1980), pp. 247–71, esp. pp. 267–68, quoted in Kohn, *Punishment by Rewards*, p. 131.
3. Erik Brynjolfsson and Andrew McAfee, *The Second Machine Age: Work, Progress, and Prosperity in a Time of Brilliant Technologies* (New York, 2014).
4. Dan Cable and Freek Vermeulen, "Why CEO Pay Should Be 100% Fixed," *Harvard Business Review* (February 23, 2016).
5. Madison Marriage and Aliya Ram, "Two Top Asset Managers Drop Staff Bonuses," *Financial Times*, August 22, 2016.
6. Jeffrey Preffer and Robert I. Sutton, "Evidence-Based Management," *Harvard Business Review* (January 2006), pp. 63–74, esp. p. 68.
7. Boris Ewenstein, Bryan Hancock, and Asmus Komm, "Ahead of the Curve: The Future of Performance Management," *McKinsey Quarterly*, no. 2 (2006), pp. 64–73, esp. p. 72.
8. Ewenstein et al., "Ahead of the Curve," pp. 67–68.
9. Tyler Cowen and Alex Tabarrok, *Modern Principles of Macroeconomics*, 3rd ed. (New York, 2014), p. 413.
10. Mark Maremont, "EpiPen Maker Dispenses Outsize Pay," *Wall Street Journal*, September 13, 2016; and Tara Parker-Pope and Rachel Rabkin Peachman, "EpiPen Price Rise Sparks Concern for Allergy Sufferers," *New York Times*, August 22, 2016.
11. Matt Levine, "Wells Fargo Opened a Couple Million Fake Accounts," Bloomberg.com, September 9, 2016; and United States of America Consumer Financial Protection Bureau, Administrative Proceeding 2016-CFPB-0015, Consent Order.
12. For other examples, see Gibbons, "Incentives in Organizations," p. 118.
13. Ferraro, Pfeffer, and Sutton, "Economics Language and Assumptions."

14. Douglas H. Frank and Tomasz Obloj, "Firm-Specific Human Capital, Organizational Incentives, and Agency Costs: Evidence from Retail Banking," *Strategic Management Journal* 35 (2014), pp. 1279–301.

15. These examples are cited in ibid., p. 1282.

16. The account that follows draws upon Amar Bhidé, "An Accident Waiting to Happen," *Critical Review* 21, nos. 2–3 (2009), pp. 211–47; and Bhidé, *A Call for Judgment: Sensible Finance for a Dynamic Economy* (New York, 2010), esp. "Introduction"; and Arnold Kling, "The Financial Crisis: Moral Failure or Cognitive Failure?" *Harvard Journal of Law and Public Policy* 33, no. 2 (2010), pp. 507–18, and Arnold Kling, *Specialization and Trade* (Washington, D.C., 2016).

17. Kling, "The Financial Crisis"; and Kling, *Specialization and Trade*, pp. 182–83.

18. Lawrence G. McDonald with Patrick Robinson, *A Colossal Failure of Common Sense: The Inside Story of the Collapse of Lehman Brothers* (New York, 2009), pp. 106–9.

19. Amar Bhidé, "Insiders and Outsiders," *Forbes*, September 24, 2008.

20. The paragraphs that follow draw upon Jerry Z. Muller, "Capitalism and Inequality: What the Right and the Left Get Wrong," *Foreign Affairs* (March–April 2013), pp. 30–51.

21. Hyman P. Minsky, "Uncertainty and the Institutional Structure of Capitalist Economies," *Journal of Economic Issues* 30, no. 2 (June 1996), pp. 357–68; Levy Economics Institute, *Beyond the Minsky Moment* (e-book, April 2012); Alfred Rappaport, *Saving Capitalism from Short-Termism* (New York, 2011).

22. On the propensity for short-termism of publicly traded companies, see John Asker, Joan Farre-Mensa, and Alexander Ljungqvist, "Corporate Investment and Stock Market Listing: A Puzzle?" *Review of Financial Studies* 28, no. 2 (2015), pp. 342–90.

23. http://www.businessinsider.com/blackrock-ceo-larry-fink-letter-to-sp-500-ceos-2016-2.

24. Klarman, *A Margin of Safety*.

25. Nelson P. Repenning and Rebecca M. Henderson, "Making the Numbers? 'Short Termism' and the Puzzle of Only Occasional Disaster," Harvard Business School Working Paper 11–33, 2010. On the negative effects of some pay-for-performance schemes on trust, employee commitment, and institutional productivity, see Michael Beer and Mark D. Cannon, "Promise and Peril in Implementing Pay-for-Performance," *Human Resources Management* 43, no. 1 (Spring 2004), pp. 3–48.

26. Michael C. Jensen, "Paying People to Lie: The Truth about the Budgeting Process," *European Financial Management* 9, no. 3 (2003), pp. 379–406.

27. Gary P. Pisano and Willy C. Shih, "Restoring American Competitiveness," *Harvard Business Review* (July 2009), pp. 11–12.

28. Yves Morieux of Boston Consulting Group, in his TED talk, "How Too Many Rules at Work Keep You from Getting Things Done," July 2015; see also Morieux and Tollman, *Six Simple Rules*.

29. Frank Knight, *Risk, Uncertainty, and Profit* (New York, 1921).

30. Isabell Welpe, "Performance Paradoxon: Erfolg braucht Uneindeutigkeit: Warum es klug ist, sich nicht auf eine Erfolgskennzahl festzulegen," *Wirtschaftswoche* July 31, 2015, p. 88.

CHAPTER 13. PHILANTHROPY AND FOREIGN AID

1. Ann Goggins Gregory and Don Howard, "The Nonprofit Starvation Cycle," *Stanford Innovation Review* (Fall 2009); and "The Overhead Myth," http://overheadmythcom.b.presscdn.com/wp-content/uploads/2013/06 /GS_OverheadMyth_Ltr_ONLINE.pdf.

2. See, for example, P. T. Bauer, *Dissent on Development* (Cambridge, Mass., 1976).

3. Mark Moyar, *Aid for Elites: Building Partner Nations and Ending Poverty through Human Capital* (Cambridge, 2016), p. 188. The entire chapter on "Measurement" is invaluable.

4. Andrew Natsios, "The Clash of the Counter-Bureaucracy and Development" (2010), http://www.cgdev.org/publication/clash-counter-bureau cracy-and-development; and Natsios, "The Foreign Aid Reform Agenda," *Foreign Service Journal* 86, no. 12 (December 2008), quoted in Moyar, *Aid for Elites*, pp. 188–89.

5. Unnamed USAID official, interviewed by Mark Moyar in 2012, and quoted in Moyar, *Aid for Elites*, p. 190.

6. Moyar, *Aid for Elites*, p. 186.

CHAPTER 14. WHEN TRANSPARENCY IS THE ENEMY OF PERFORMANCE: POLITICS, DIPLOMACY, INTELLIGENCE, AND MARRIAGE

1. Moshe Halbertal, *Concealment and Revelation: Esotericism in Jewish Thought and Its Philosophical Implications,* trans. Jackie Feldman (Princeton, 2007), pp. 142–43.

2. Tom Daschle, foreword to Jason Grumet, *City of Rivals: Restoring the Glorious Mess of American Democracy* (New York, 2014), p. x.

3. See on this Jonathan Rauch, "How American Politics Went Insane," *The Atlantic*, July–August, 2016; Jonathan Rauch, "Why Hillary Clinton Needs to be Two-Faced," *New York Times*, October 22, 2016; and Matthew Yglesias, "Against Transparency," *Vox*, September 6, 2016.

4. Cass R. Sunstein, "Output Transparency vs. Input Transparency," August 18, 2016, https://papers.ssrn.com/sol3/papers.cfm?abstract_id=2826009.

5. Wikipedia, "Chelsea Manning."

6. Christian Stöcker, "Leak at WikiLeaks: A Dispatch Disaster in Six Acts," *Spiegel Online*, September 1, 2011.

7. Halbertal, *Concealment and Revelation*, p. 164.

8. Joel Brenner, *Glass Houses: Privacy, Secrecy, and Cyber Insecurity in a Transparent World* (New York, 2013), p. 210.

CHAPTER 15. UNINTENDED BUT PREDICTABLE NEGATIVE CONSEQUENCES

1. Ravitch, *The Death and Life of the Great American School System*, p. 161; Stewart, *The Management Myth*, p. 54.

2. Holmström and Milgrom, "Multitask Principal-Agent Analyses."

3. Merton, "Unanticipated Consequences and Kindred Sociological Ideas: A Personal Gloss," p. 296.

4. Morieux and Tollman, *Six Simple Rules*, pp. 6–16.

5. Lilford and Pronovost, "Using Hospital Mortality Rates to Judge Hospital Performance."

6. Berwick, "The Toxicity of Pay for Performance."

7. On this topic, see George A. Akerlof and Rachel E. Kranton, *Identity Economics: How Our Identities Shape Our Work, Wages, and Well-Being* (Princeton, 2010), chap. 5, "Identity and the Economics of Organizations."

8. Berwick, "The Toxicity of Pay for Performance."

9. Edmund Phelps, *Mass Flourishing: How Grassroots Innovation Created Jobs, Challenge and Change* (Princeton, 2013), p. 269.

10. Similarly, Scott, *Seeing Like a State*, p. 313.

11. According to Dale Jorgenson of Harvard, the only source of growth of total factor productivity was in IT-producing industries. Dale W. Jorgenson, Mun Ho, and Jon D. Samuels, "The Outlook for U.S. Economic Growth," in Brink Lindsey (ed.), *Understanding the Growth Slowdown*

(Washington, D.C., 2015). On how behavioral metrics in human resources sap initiative, see Lutz, *Car Guys vs. Bean Counters*, pp. ix–x.

CHAPTER 16. WHEN AND HOW TO USE METRICS: A CHECKLIST

1. Young et al., "Financial Incentives, Professional Values and Performance," *Journal of Organizational Behavior* 33 (2012), pp. 964–83, esp. p. 969.
2. Thomas Kochan, commentary on "Promise and Peril in Implementing Pay-for-Performance," *Human Resources Management* 43, no. 1 (Spring 2004), pp. 35–37.
3. J. Matthew Austin, Elizabeth A. McGlynn, and Peter J. Pronovost, "Fostering Transparency in Outcomes, Quality, Safety, and Costs," *JAMA* 316, no. 16 (October 25, 2016), pp. 1661–62.
4. B. S. Frey and M. Osterloh, *Successful Management by Motivation. Balancing Intrinsic and Extrinsic Incentives* (Heidelberg, 2002).
5. Kling, *Specialization and Trade*, p. 33.

INDEX

abstract and formulaic knowledge, 59–60

"Academic Ranking of World Universities," 75–76

accountability, 3–6; advocates of, 17–18, 113; growth in applications of, 63–64; quest for numerical metrics of, 40

Acemoglu, Daron, 72

achievement gap, 20, 91, 96–99

Adelphia, 144

Affordable Care Act, 104, 114–15

Afghanistan War, 131–34

agency capitalism, 148

American Recovery and Reinvestment Act, 94

Annals of Internal Medicine, 115–16

Arnold, Matthew, 12, 30–31, 92

authority, suspicion of, 41

Autor, David, 72

Baumol, William, 44

Bell, Daniel, 33

benchmarks, 6

Benghazi investigations, 162

Berwick, Donald, 119–20, 172

Bin Laden, Osama, 171

BlackRock, 149

Blair, Tony, 114

Bodies, 2–3

bounded rationality, 45

Bowen, William G., 44

Bratton, William J., 126

Bresch, Heather, 141, 142

Burns, Ed, 1, 129

Bush, George W., 11, 64, 89, 90

business and finance: financial crisis of 2008 and, 145–47; other dysfunctions in, 150–51; short-termism in, 147–50; when paying for performance works, and when it doesn't, in, 137–45

business schools, 12–13, 138–39

Cable, Dan, 138

Campbell, Donald T., 19, 127

Campbell's Law, 19, 24, 80, 93, 127

capitalism, 87, 172; agency, 148

case selection bias, 117–18. *See also* creaming

Centers for Medicare and Medicaid, 112, 119

cheating, 24

Chronicle of Higher Education, The, 76

Circle, The, 140

civil rights law, 42

Cleveland Clinic, 107–8, 110–11, 117

Clinton, Bill, 64, 90

Clinton, Hillary, 162

Coleman Report, 98

colleges and universities. *See* higher education

Collini, Stefan, 40

Commission on the Future of Higher Education, 11